AUTISM

THE GOOD, THE BAD AND THE WONDERFUL.

BY:

SHARON JEACOCK

PROLOGUE

I started to write this journal as part of my ongoing therapy, but then COVID-19 and lockdown hit, and my journal was getting longer and longer. I decided to turn it into a memoir to help raise much-needed awareness for special educational needs, disabilities and mental health.

The fight for what is right and that to which you are entitled, the fight to be heard, and the fight to be believed plunged my family into the depths of utter despair. Once we were believed and had a diagnosis, the fight didn't get any easier.

The system failed my son in the most dreadful, heartbreaking way for years, and an independent watchdog proved this.

My son, a frightened, young, autistic boy, was treated appallingly by a person who was meant to be helping him. I was so low and vulnerable after years of pleading for help that when help eventually came, I myself was groomed and sexually assaulted by a so-called professional.

This is a book of hope and shows that things can get better, even when you think they won't and when you can't see a way out, there is light at the end of that long tunnel.

If this book can help just one family going through something similar, then it will be worth it. Some names have been changed to protect the identities of the innocent and the not-so-innocent!

Stay strong, and keep fighting for what is right!

CHAPTER ONE

The 4th of December 2002 arrived, and I was feeling excited, apprehensive, and extremely nervous. That morning, I was to go into the hospital for my Caesarean section and finally meet the newest member of our little family. We already had Joseph, who had just turned three the day before, and he was beside himself with excitement at the thought of meeting and becoming a big brother to his new sibling. My husband Kenny and I kissed him goodbye and left him with his Nan, promising that we would let him know later whether it was a boy or a girl. And when he could come visit and bring the cuddly teddy bear that he so wanted to give to the new baby.

At 11 am, our son Charlie was delivered safe and sound, looking absolutely perfect, and I fell in love instantly. My husband was just as in awe as I was, and once I had been taken to recovery, he started to ring around friends and family, Nan and Joseph being at the top of the list. That evening, Kenny brought Joseph to meet his new baby brother, and he couldn't keep his eyes off of him and cried and cried when it was time for his dad to take him home. After a few days, we were discharged, and soon life settled into a routine of feeding, winding, and nappy changes. Joseph and Charlie were very different babies. Joseph was very colicky, always hungry, and did not sleep well. He had only weighed 5 lbs at birth, and his constant hunger meant he soon put on weight, whereas Charlie was very quiet, rarely cried, and had to be woken up for his feeds. I remember thinking at the time that this was going to be a piece of cake!

The months rolled by, and the 3rd and 4th of December 2003 came around, being Joseph's fourth and Charlie's first birthdays, respectively. Soon after, we were called to our doctors' surgery for Charlie's one-year check-up. As we sat in the doctor's office, my GP said to me, "Is Charlie always like this?" I smiled and said, "Yes, he is the quiet one." The doctor said, "I would like to see Charlie again in six months' time if he is still the same." I did not think much of it at the time, as I always believed that you shouldn't compare siblings or any child to each other. In hindsight, I wish that I had listened to my GP; it would have saved us so many years of struggling and fighting for my son's rights. But as it was, I just carried on thinking my now toddler was just very shy and quiet and liked to have things done in a particular order.

He always had to have the same cereal bowl with the same rabbit spoon, for instance. If I could not find it straight away, I could feel panic rising in me as Charlie would be beside himself, the poor boy; it was just awful. Even to this day, he still has to have his own cutlery and always the same ones. Shortly after Charlie turned two, I noticed that he would react in the exact same way with his clothes too. He could not bear anything with labels on and could not tolerate any type of transfer on his T-shirts; even the seams in socks used to aggravate him, and denim jeans were out of the question. If I hadn't put his clothes on exactly right the first time, then he would cry and screech and kick his legs out at me and get into such a temper, and on more than one occasion, made himself sick. It was just all too unbearable and painful for him and also for me. I found it very upsetting and frustrating as I thought it must be me, that I was doing things wrong, and that I couldn't make my child happy and comfortable. He lived in fleece shorts and plain v-neck tops all the time, no matter the season, but that was OK as long as he was comfortable. I let him wear whatever felt right to him. However, he would still cry and fidget dreadfully at the slightest feeling of discomfort. I tried to pacify him, but this had next to no effect at all. It became extremely frustrating for us all when we were in a hurry to get out of the door for an appointment or in a rush to get Joseph to school or pick him up. Then, it would take so much longer, having to make sure that

4

I got the shoes and socks on perfectly the first time; otherwise, the long process of starting again would begin. It got to the stage where we dreaded getting an invitation to a party or wedding, as finding Charlie suitable clothes for such events was nigh on impossible and so overwhelming for us all that it was easier to turn down the invitation, which was so sad.

I was still putting this behaviour down to the terrible twos that I had heard so much about, but Joseph was never that unhappy or regimented at the same age. Around the age of two and a half, Charlie started to line up his toy cars and lorries in perfectly straight lines and always in the exact same order. One morning, I was hovering over the lounge floor, and I accidentally disturbed the perfect line; well, you would have thought the world had ended. Poor Charlie was beside himself, and no amount of me trying to put it right would help calm him down. I couldn't even cuddle him, as he hated to be hugged or cuddled, and that is the one thing you want to do when you are a mum. Charlie developed the same obsession with stones and sticks as well, and he would bring them home, his pockets stuffed with them. My husband and I found this behaviour very upsetting and started to worry that something could very well be wrong, but we decided to give it time; after all, he was still only two and a half years old.

Every autumn, I would go across the fields blackberrying, and this carried on once I had my boys. Joseph eagerly put his wellies on, and I would sit Charlie in his buggy, and off we would go to find our goodies. Joseph walked happily beside me, swinging his little bucket and so excited at the thought of picking some berries and eating a good few too! Whereas Charlie had his bucket on his lap and didn't even look up at the fruit that I was showing him. I was trying my hardest to drum up some enthusiasm, and I so wanted him to enjoy the experience and have fun as well, but poor Charlie just still sat with his head down, almost looking lost and depressed. It was the same when we went to the local play park or even shopping; he didn't seem to notice things, and when I tried to point things out to him, his expression remained the same.

It was an unusually warm September, so one Saturday, we decided it would be nice to make the most of the early September sunshine. We loaded up the car and set off for a rare day out to the seaside. Things went very calmly, and we all had such a wonderful day doing all the usual things: making sandcastles, paddling in the sea, and eating candy floss. Both boys thoroughly enjoyed themselves, and all too soon, it was time to leave the beach. My husband Kenny said, "Come on then, we can get chips and ice cream before we head off home." That was all the telling Joseph needed as his little face lit up. He couldn't wait to get going and have his favourite treat of sausage and chips, followed by ice cream. We were all packed up and ready to go and said, "Come on, Charlie, time to go," but Charlie had other ideas and would not budge. No amount of coaxing would persuade him otherwise, as he was far too busy lining up pebbles, which were his new favourite thing.

He was absolutely mesmerised by them, and with the waves lapping the shore, we said, "Goodbye then, Charlie," and started to walk away. Of course, we would never have left him or gone too far, so we couldn't see him, but this tactic had always worked with Joseph as it normally would with most other children. We got further away, and still, Charlie didn't look around once. I think we could have gone, and he still would not have realised. He was playing away, still lining up pebbles. We stood and observed him for around three minutes, although it seemed so much longer. We thought he would suddenly realise, look for us, and come running; however, we knew that was not going to happen. Kenny went back to fetch him to bring him up the beach to me and his buggy.

My goodness, what a traumatic state he got himself into. He was almost sick and bright red in the face, kicking and hitting out at both of us. He was still carrying his bucket of stones, and he certainly wasn't letting that go, however upset he got. I don't know how he held onto them without spilling them, as his arms and legs were flying all over the place. By now, people were staring and tutting and wondering what on earth was wrong with him. I remember thinking to myself at the time that I hoped nobody thought we were kidnapping this little boy.

Eventually, he calmed down, and we managed to buy the chips and ice cream and then began the long journey home. Both boys slept all the way, totally exhausted. Looking back, poor Joseph never complained or made a fuss when his brother had one of these episodes; he just seemed to take it in his stride and accept things as they were.

Occasionally, in those early days, he would look and catch my eye in the midst of Charlie having a meltdown and raise his eyes. Joseph was very patient with him and was such an excellent help to me. I would find out just how much of a help he was to become to me years later.

In September, before Charlie turned three, it was time for him to start at the village playgroup for two afternoons per week. I was really looking forward to this as Joseph had absolutely loved it and enjoyed all of his sessions there. It definitely got him ready for the next stage of his early years in primary school, which was located just next door to the playgroup, so it was ideal and worked very well. I knew the staff, and they were all very kind and made the sessions such good fun. I took Charlie for a visit as I had done with his brother, and all went well as I held Charlie's hand and showed him the peg that would eventually have his name above it, where he could hang his coat.

One of the stipulations was that the toddlers had to be toilet-trained before they could attend the playgroup. This was no problem at all for us; Charlie had been a breeze to toilet-train, as he couldn't bear his nappy being even slightly damp. I was constantly checking his nappy as he felt wet, but sometimes it was just a bit of sweat or the tiniest bit of urine, so being toilet-trained, he was good to go.

He was scheduled to attend the sessions on a Tuesday and a Wednesday afternoon, so that weekend, I went into town and brought him the things the teachers had said he would need: wellington boots, black plimsolls and a backpack — featuring Charlie's favourite, Bob the Builder. When Charlie got home, I showed him his new things, and we were looking forward to the big day. It would do Charlie a world of good to mix with other children his age and make some friends; it was just what he needed, or so I had hoped, but it didn't exactly work out that way...

CHAPTER TWO

For the first session of playgroup, mums or dads were invited to stay for a settling-in period to make things easier for the new children. Our first session went OK, although Charlie stuck to me like glue, which didn't worry me too much at the time as he seemed content to sit on my lap and preferred to watch the other boys and girls play rather than join in. They were playing with dolls, cars, and trains in the Wendy's house. They had a large box of dressing-up clothes, and there was always something going on to entertain them. About twenty minutes before the session was to end, the lady in charge told us that it was part of the routine to have a snack and a drink before they went to sit on the carpeted area to sing some songs and then listen to a story. It would help to wind the children down before their parents came to pick them up. The snack was generally fruit bread or a cheese biscuit with a drink of juice.

On the first occasion, Charlie refused to eat or drink anything. I put it down to nervousness with it being his first time at playgroup and being so new to him. Soon, it was time to go home, and Charlie fell asleep, worn out from his new adventure, albeit spent sitting on my knee! When it was time for the next session, a couple of days later, we went into the playgroup, and almost immediately, Charlie clung to me tightly.

I took him inside the main room and showed him all of the interesting things that the teachers had put out, ready for all the little ones to enjoy. There were several tables, all with different activities on them; one had cars, another had books, or you could go onto the paint table or play with playdough. Charlie gravitated towards the water table, as he loved the feel of water running over his hands and through his fingers. This particular water table had a wheel that you could pour water on with a small plastic cup.

Next to the cup was a funnel and little boats, all manner of things to keep small hands occupied.

The mums had started to gingerly edge their way to the door, ready to make their escape. I thought for a few seconds that I should perhaps do the same — as I had done when I had left Joseph for the first time — but I didn't just want to leave him without warning or without saying anything to him, so very gently I put my hand on his shoulder and said "mummy is going to pop home for a little while, but will be back soon, and then you can tell me all about the fun you've had," without any warning Charlie started to cry and shake his head, motioning a no! He looked so distraught; it must have been so traumatic for him.

It was a huge thing for a little boy to have his mum leave him with strangers. I asked the manager what I should do, and she reassured me that it was all perfectly normal. She could almost guarantee that once I had gone, he would stop crying and find a little friend or a toy that would take his mind off me and would be absolutely fine. I had great faith in the manager as she was very experienced and had always been so good with Joseph. He had barely given me a second glance when he had gone on his first afternoon, and it had pleased me to think that he must feel comfortable and happy there, having lots of fun.

I was always pleased to go and fetch Joseph as he would wait on the story mat with the other boys and girls, and when the teacher said, "Here is your mummy, Joseph. You can go," he would jump up with a happy grin and come hurtling towards me saying, "mummy, mummy, that's my mummy." Hearing those words would warm my heart and make me smile, and I would scoop him up and give him a kiss and a big squeeze. Joseph loved it at playgroup and would be beside himself with excitement as he told me all about what he had done. So, with the teacher's reassuring words, I felt a bit better and, as she had advised, slowly filed out with the other mums. I had a chat with some of them once we were outside, which was nice because I already knew most of them as we had older children who had attended the playgroup together and were now together in the school.

Once I got home, the house seemed very quiet, with only me in it. For the previous three years, I had always had a little one around to keep me busy and on my toes! I thought I should make the most of the next couple of hours. I probably caught up on some jobs around the house or prepared things for our evening meal, nothing earth-shattering, but it made me feel on top of things and like I was coping. It also kept my wandering to Charlie, though he was never far away from my thoughts. The two hours soon whizzed by, so I made my way across the road to pick Charlie up. When I was let into the playgroup, I was not expecting the same gush of excitement as I had gotten from Joseph, but I was so looking forward to seeing his little face and hearing all about what he had been up to.

What greeted me when I entered the room was a very sorrowful little boy sitting on the story mat with his little legs crossed, looking very forlorn, and I just knew at that moment that he had not enjoyed himself. The playgroup teacher said cheerfully, "You can go, Charlie, your mummy is here." He didn't run to me or smile; he just waddled over to me with a kind of deadpan expression. He put his arms up for me to pick him up, and once I had him in my arms, he clung onto me for dear life and buried his little face in the crook of my neck. I could feel the heat coming off him and the wetness from a combination of sweat and tears. He never told me about his afternoon despite my asking. He never even said whether he had a nice, fun time or not; he would just look at me and not say anything, and the more I asked, the angrier and grumpy he became. I felt the tears pricking at my eyes and tried to ignore the knot I had in my stomach. However, I wouldn't be able to ignore it for much longer!

The following week's visit arrived, and off we went again. As I suspected, when I went to leave, he didn't want me to go, but the teacher said, "Just go; he will be fine." I asked her if he had been fine the week before, and I was slightly reassured again when she said, "Yes, he was fine, very quiet, and preferred to play on his own; he was no trouble at all." So off I went, feeling apprehensive, but knowing I had to be strong and that it would be for Charlie's benefit in the long run. I hadn't been in long, just long enough for the kettle to boil, and the telephone rang. "Hello," I said. It was Charlie's teacher, and before she could say anything, I could hear Charlie crying loudly in the background. She said, "I'm sorry to ring you, but can you come back as there is no settling him." I went straight over, and the sight that was before me is one I shall never forget. The kind teachers were trying their utmost to pacify him with cuddles and cajole him with toys to try and distract him, but all to no avail.

My poor boy was in such a state, crying, screaming, and bright red in his chubby little face. His beautiful wispy curls were stuck flat to his head with sweat, snot was running down his nose, dribble mixed with vomit coming from his mouth. He could hardly breathe from all the crying; oh my goodness, my poor, poor boy. I scooped him up into my arms from the teacher's lap and gathered his belongings. I thanked the staff for calling me so promptly and left as quickly as I could. We tried several more times to get Charlie into playgroup, and on every occasion, Charlie kicked and screamed all the way.

The poor boy must have been beyond terrified, but from what I was being told, it was the right thing to do, and I so wanted him to fit in and be happy. In the end, it just wasn't working, and I lost count of the times I was phoned to come back over. In the end, it was decided that I could stay with Charlie to see how things went, and I was very pleased to see that he was so much calmer and settled with me being there. He still preferred to sit quietly, playing with the toy cars or trains and the water table. Every now and then, he would look around the room for me to make sure I was still there. He even made a friend who was, and still is, a lovely lad. There was a rota in the playgroup where the mums or dads were asked to put their names down to take a turn and help out when and if they could, usually a couple of times a month. As I was always there, I got to know the mums and dads well, and it was nice to chat with them about everyday normal things. It was a lovely, relaxed atmosphere in the group, and it felt wonderful to be part of something.

Once Charlie was three, he was eligible to start going to playgroup for the morning sessions instead of getting ready to start at the early years unit within the school. I put Charlie down for three mornings a week with the plan that it could be increased over time. Unfortunately, that didn't happen, and we kept it to the three mornings, but Charlie was coping well as long as I was in his line of sight, and having his friend with him helped no end. The December that Charlie turned four meant his time at playgroup was coming to an end. In January, he was due to start in the early years unit. The last session at the playgroup was good, as they had a little party. The parents started to filter in to collect their children and to say goodbye to the teachers.

A lot of the parents had brought gifts for the staff, as you very often do. I was very surprised when I was presented with cards and gifts; they actually thought that I worked there! I explained, feeling very embarrassed, and tried to give the gifts back, but they all insisted that I kept them; I felt very awkward about this, almost as if I had cheated them out of it. I was always pleased when the school holidays came around, as it was a break for all of us. I was starting to get very tired and tearful, and would often feel niggly and fretful about things.

I made an appointment with our family doctor as Charlie had started to fall over a lot, which resulted in him hurting himself. He often complained of feeling soreness in his knees, back, and hips. The doctor referred us to the local children's hospital in Oxford, where it was explained that they would carry out a series of tests to try and determine what was going on. The tests consisted of checking urine and blood, a physical exam of his limbs, and finally, a sweat test. It did not go to plan at all. I had to apply some numbing cream in the crooks of Charlie's arms and then wrap them in a type of cling film.

That part went surprisingly well, and it wasn't long after we all got called through to see a junior doctor. He went through some questions with us and then said, Right then, if you can lay Charlie down on the bed, I can take the blood samples. "I was helping Charlie to lay back on the bed all the time, explaining why I was doing it. He was resisting me, so the doctor tried to lay him back as well, which just made a bad situation a whole lot worse. She then instructed my husband to hold down Charlie's shoulders while the doctor and I had his legs, but it made Charlie worse, and by then, he had gotten to the point of no return. She kept saying, "Hold him steady; I need to take his blood." Charlie was getting very flustered and red in the face, and I was extremely concerned and felt at that point the exam should be stopped, but again, me being me, I did as I was asked. I kept saying "I'm sorry," but it fell on deaf ears, and she kept tutting and sighing.

In the end, she got cross and said to me, "For goodness's sake, have you ever tried disciplining your child." I did not know what to say to her, and I could feel my face burning and pulsing and the tears threatening to come again. She wrote on her paperwork, 'unable to examine due to child's behaviour', and with that, walked out and left us in the room in some sort of quiet shock at what had just happened. I still remember that doctor's name to this day and hope if she ever goes on to have children, that will teach her patience. Eventually, we saw a lovely doctor/consultant who examined Charlie and did numerous tests, all stress-free.

Our son had a condition called hypermobility, and we left armed with lots of information on what we could do to help him and what to expect. I felt teary and very down, as I had so much of late, and it was all getting too much. I was so tired, having been in playgroup for a couple of years, looking after my young family with Charlie having his little ways. I was finding my job at the nursing home too much. I absolutely loved my job and had been a care assistant at the same care home for eighteen years, but something had to give… and it did.

CHAPTER THREE

I left school in May 1988, just before my sixteenth birthday in June. We were allowed to leave as long as we went back for any exams and then to go in for our results.

I was never very academic at school, but didn't come out of it too badly, with a few passes and two distinctions. I had got my City and Guilds certificates, which was pretty amazing as I was a proper chatterbox, but I was never disruptive in lessons and was always polite and willing to help the teachers when they needed an errand run or something similar. I was, in fact, a very shy girl until I got to know someone, and then I wouldn't shut up! I had two really good friends in my year. We were the very best of friends and would hang out together in and out of school, enjoying sleepovers, trips into town on the bus, and just generally listening to the latest music and talking about the latest boy we liked the look of, but most of all enjoying a good old giggle and gossip, the typical teenage girl type of thing. We all promised that once we left school, we would keep in touch and be best friends for life, as you do when you are that age.

The last day of school had at last arrived, and I could not wait! When I heard that bell signalling the day's end, I jumped up and bounded out of class without a second thought. I skipped and laughed with my two friends to the bus stop, and I was daydreaming all the way home about what the long summer would have in store for us all. By this time I had a boyfriend who was a couple of years older than me, he was into his cars and sometimes used to pick me up from school. I felt like the bee's knees getting into his car. We spent so much time together, and along with our friends, we went ice skating, although I preferred to watch from the sidelines as I had absolutely no sense of balance. I didn't mind one bit, though, as I loved to watch them skate, and there was always really loud music playing, which added to the atmosphere.

Afterwards, we would all go to McDonald's or Wimpy. I was just over the moon to think I had the whole summer with my boyfriend and friends. I was just about at bursting point by the time I arrived back in the village and ran home to my mum. As I burst through the door, I was gushing over everything I had planned. I went straight to my bedroom and clawed off my starchy, itchy uniform for the very last time, leaving it in a heap on the floor, quickly dressing in my normal clothes and blasting out Wham! Or Madonna.

I felt positively gleeful. That feeling was cut very short very quickly as my dear dad had other plans and ideas for me that summer, and in his exact words, "I'm not having you sitting idle all summer," he then announced that first thing on Monday morning he would be driving me around local businesses in town to find me a job! I was beyond mad and "Oh no Dad, please at least let me have the summer off." That did not cut any ice with him at all, and I remember having a major sulk and cry in my room, thinking, "Right, that's it, I'm moving out," then it dawned on me that I would need money, and to get the money I would need a job.

I soon calmed down and accepted the fate that awaited me on Monday morning. It wouldn't be so bad. I thought I could still see my boyfriend and friends after work and on weekends. At the time, my dad was off of work poorly; he had terrible stomach pain and no appetite, so he had lost a lot of weight. He had to be taken into hospital by ambulance as he had been in agony. Our doctor was treating him for irritable bowel syndrome. He gave him some painkillers and medicine to stop his stomach spasms, which seemed to help a bit, but he was still signed off of work. First thing Monday morning, my dad drove me around the town. We had gone into several places with no luck as they did not have any vacancies, which of course secretly delighted me, then we found ourselves at the Little Chef restaurant just outside the town. They had a vacancy for a waitress and offered me the position. I thought there were worse places I could work, and I quickly warmed to the idea of being a waitress.

We got back to the car, and my dad said, "No way are you working there." I can't remember why he was so against it. So that was that. We tried one last place on an industrial estate, and this time, I was to go in on my own, which terrified me. I remember saying, "Can't I just ring them, or better still, write them a letter?" Dad said, "No, it's much better to go in person as they will think more of you." So off I went in typical sixteen-year-old awkwardness. I was mortified when I opened the door to what felt like dozens and dozens of women's eyes burning into me. A very smart middle-aged lady came over and said, "Can I help you?" I said very meekly, "Could I please speak to the boss, as I'm looking for a job?" The lady fetched her boss, a young man in a suit, and he invited me into his office and asked me what it was that I was looking for. I just about managed to speak or squeak out the words, "I would very much like a job if one is available, please." He smiled at me and asked me various questions about myself and my education, and after what seemed like ages but probably only ten minutes, he said, "I would like to give you a job, as we do have a vacancy." I said, "Oh, thank you so much, that's great!" still having no idea what the actual job was that I had been offered! It turned out it was a promotional company, where customers would collect tokens or labels off cereal boxes or margarine tubs and send them to us with their address and twenty-four pence for postage and packing in exchange for a mop, houseplant or something similar.

I settled in well, and of course, my dad was thrilled. My job entailed two weeks of opening, sorting the money and making sure that they had sent the right amount of tokens. I would send the addresses to the girls on the factory floor to pack the gifts up and place them in a big crate ready for posting. After two weeks, we would all swap. I much preferred it when I was opening the envelopes of tokens and money as I really enjoyed reading the letters that some of the customers had included; some had even put in pictures of their pets too. I just loved it and found it interesting to hear about people's lives. Looking back now, I think that maybe these people were lonely and excited to write us a letter.

Others had sent in the twenty-four pence and tokens but no address, so we had no idea where to send the gift. While others sent in the tokens and addresses but no money. Sometimes, I used to let them through as I felt sorry for them, but then, of course, when I came to cash up at the end of the day, it didn't tally, so I would end up putting the money in myself. I really enjoyed working there, but unfortunately, after a year I was told that the firm would be moving some miles away and as I couldn't drive I didn't move with them, so I had to leave.

I managed to get another job more or less immediately. My next-door neighbour had approached my parents and me to ask if I would be interested in being a care assistant at a local nursing home. This was a job I really did not want, not because I was squeamish or afraid of hard work, but because I never thought I could do this particular job. Initially, I thought, OK, I will give it a go, and if I really don't like it, then I can always look for something else. I absolutely loved it and was there for eighteen happy years, and it was a big part of my life.

I started in June, just before my seventeenth birthday, and I was so nervous. I was to do the 7 am to 3 pm shift, so I had to be at work by at least 6. 45 am so we could get a handover from the night shift. I was introduced to the deputy manager that morning, and she explained to me that usually I would shadow an experienced carer for a week or so or until they thought I was confident and competent enough to be let loose on my own list of residents.

However, on this day, the home was extremely short-staffed. I was told, "I'm sorry, but I am going to have to throw you in at the deep end." Well, that very nearly had me turning on my heels and running for the hills. She smiled at me and said, "Don't worry; I shall show you how to wash and dress the residents and how to clean their dentures or teeth if they have any." She continued, "I will show you catheter and conveen care another day, along with incontinence care and how to bathe the residents'." I hadn't even heard of catheters and conveens, let alone what I was supposed to do with them! One thing that had to be right was the hospital corners when bed-making. I soon got the hang of doing them and still do them to this day.

We were so busy that first day, and they seemed very pleased with me as they said that I had taken to it like a duck to water, although I didn't feel like I had. It was a massive home with around eighty bedrooms, it had been an RAF officers' mess in the war, and it had a huge dining room and day rooms and a lovely welcoming reception area. The home was split into two wings, one to the left and one to the right. I never thought that I would ever remember all of the residents' names, let alone who was who, when the bell system used to light up, indicating somebody needed our assistance. I was getting a lift home that first day from my neighbour and was told to wait for her in reception. I was pleased to have a sit-down and rest after my busy first day.

That day, there was a lot of activity in the home, as the next day was the annual fête on the grounds. People were buzzing around, making sure that all was going as planned. Lots of the staff had stalls to run, and the kitchen staff were busy making scones and cupcakes to sell on the day, along with tea or coffee. All of the residents' relatives had been invited, and it had been advertised locally in the hope that more people would come from the local town and villages. I had heard some of the staff saying that a marquee was to be delivered by the army. The plan was that they would drop the marquee off and return the following morning to put it up. I was really looking forward to the next day and being involved in the fête.

I was still sitting waiting for my lift home when a lady came into reception walking with her hands behind her back, looking very important. She was elderly, and I presumed that she was maybe a volunteer of some sort as she asked me if she could help me. I said, "No, thank you, I am just waiting for my lift," to which she replied, "That's fine, let me know if you need anything," and she sat down behind a desk. Then I saw out of the window a very large army truck coming up the long drive towards the home. Immediately, I thought that it must be the marquee. The important-looking elderly lady sprung up from her seat and said, "What's this, then?" I replied, "Oh, it must be the marquee for the fête," she said, "No, that's all been cancelled." I remember feeling a bit disappointed at that but thought that there was probably a good reason for it as everyone had worked so hard to arrange it; maybe we were going to be short-staffed again.

One of the army men came into the foyer and was swiftly sent on his way by the important-looking lady saying, "It's all off, take it away, we don't need it here, thank you!" Are you sure?" the man answered, before then looking in my direction for some explanation, "well, I guess it must be." He looked very puzzled, but before he could say anything else, he was told, "Go on then, off you go," and he went.

I didn't give it another thought and arrived for my shift early the following morning. We were told to remind the residents of the fete and ask what they would like to wear for the great event, as on these occasions, they often would like to wear their Sunday best. I was feeling confused as I was still thinking that it had been cancelled, but I concluded that there must have been a change of plan.

At around 10 am, the deputy and the other staff members were looking very flustered and kept looking at their fob watches, saying, "Where on earth is the army with the marquee," someone else said that it was supposed to be here yesterday! This made me even more confused until a thought suddenly came into my mind, closely followed by a cold fear washing over me, and my legs went to jelly. It was dawning on me rapidly that maybe this important-looking volunteer was actually a very confused resident! Oh no! Please, no. Just as I've found a job I like, I am going to get the sack on the spot for being so stupid. In the end, I confided in another member of staff about what had happened, apologising profusely! Thank goodness, in the end, it all turned out well, and we all had a good laugh about it, and the army returned and saved the day. It was explained to me later, once the staff had narrowed down who the lady was, that she was indeed very confused and thought that the home belonged to her and we were her staff. Well, she certainly had me fooled! A few more incidents like this happened over the years, but thankfully, I had grown wiser. Stories like this one are partly what made the job so enjoyable.

We all got along so well. It was like having an extended family, which I found a huge comfort in as in September 1989, my dear dad passed away after a short battle with cancer. The weakness and pain that he had been experiencing since the summer had turned out to be colon cancer that had spread throughout his body. He died very peacefully at home with my mum and me by his side, at forty-three he was so young and my poor mum was only thirty-nine and already a widow. I was seventeen and was so worried about my mum and how she would cope. I felt scared as to what would happen, but I kept all my worry internalised so as not to add to Mum's grief. I was going to have to be strong now, as was my mum. I was so upset about my dad, and we were both going to miss him very much. My job really helped, and I worked hard and picked things up well, like taking blood pressure and learning to do the residents' observations, along with filling in fluid charts to make sure that they remained hydrated, keeping toilet charts to make sure that things were working as they should be, and of course the looking after the catheters and fitting of conveens. It wasn't half as daunting as I had first thought when I started.

After I had been at the nursing home for four years, I got a promotion to senior carer. It meant a lot more responsibility, as I would be in charge of my own floor of residents and staff. I would have to do the medication and make sure it was administered and signed for correctly, be in charge of doctors' and district nurses' rounds, and give enemas, suppositories and bladder washes. For the diabetics, I had to do a pinprick blood test to check their sugar levels in order to give the correct insulin dose. Most of all, I liked doing the dressings of wounds, and we had some pretty nasty leg ulcers to deal with over the years.

A fellow senior carer and I went to a hospital in Oxford to do some training on the different dressings, which was very interesting, and we were able to obtain our wound care certificate so we could carry on doing them in the home under the direction of the local district nurse. I was only 21, and it was a lot of responsibility, and it was starting to worry me. I could feel that I wasn't enjoying my job quite as much as before. I struggled for two more years, but in the end, I found it just too much. I had a talk with my manager, who was so understanding and allowed me to go back to being a care assistant. She asked if I would be willing to continue doing the blood pressure and dressings; of course, I said yes!

I had split up with my boyfriend and had been dating a lovely man named Kenny, who was ten years older than me, not that that mattered one bit. In time, we got married at the village church, and some of the more able residents were driven over in the home's minibus to see us both in our finery, which was lovely. We both had a fantastic day with all our friends and family. I fell pregnant with Joseph a couple of years later, went on maternity leave, and had our baby boy. I had three months off and went back to the home on the night shift, which was from 9 pm to 7 am. I couldn't do days as we had no childcare, so it worked well with Kenny working in the day and me at night. It was tiring; when I got home, all I wanted to do was sleep, but with a baby, that was nigh on impossible, so I slept here and there when Joseph took a nap.

I fell pregnant again with Charlie two years later. I couldn't do the night shift anymore as it was far too tiring; fortunately, I was able to do the late shift, 6 pm till midnight twice a week, and every other weekend back on the day shift. Once I had Charlie, I continued with that shift pattern, and it worked really well. By the time Charlie was almost four, he was really struggling, as was I, so with an extremely heavy heart and after eighteen happy years, my time at the care home came to an end. Something had to give; little did I know that it was to be the beginning of one hell of a time and one hell of a fight that was to last years! This was the start of a spiral of events that would nearly break me.

CHAPTER FOUR

So now I had left the nursing home, I needed to find a job with fewer hours and less responsibility, so I could concentrate on getting the help that Charlie needed. By this time, Charlie was four and had started in the early years unit at the village school. It was all going very well as his little friend from playgroup had gone up with him, which had helped the transition no end. I relaxed slightly and thought that everything would work out OK, I could feel the old me slowly coming back, and I got a cleaning job for two hours Monday to Friday in the village pub.

The hours were ideal being nine till eleven so it fitted in with getting the boys to school so well. I then took over the role as booking secretary at our local sports and social club which again was ideal as I could more or less fit the hours in while the boys were in school, a good few months had passed and whilst Charlie was still challenging at home if things didn't go his way, at least school life seemed on an even keel so when Charlie's teacher came out of his class wanting to speak to one afternoon my stomach did its usual ice-cold flipping over, and I thought 'oh no what's happened I could tell by her face that it wasn't to tell what a little angel he had been, I did my best to smile at her through my nerves of what she was going to say, apparently on numerous occasions the teacher had caught Charlie trying to smuggle home a crayon, car, stone from the playfield or small twig, but today it had been a piece Lego that had made its way into Charlie's pocket, well my heart sank, and I was apologising profusely, the teacher quite rightly was very cross with Charlie as she classed it as stealing which it was in a way, but Charlie wasn't doing it to steal, I felt it was more of a comfort thing as he formed such attachments to things and in particular to his beloved stones and cars, and it was so very difficult to explain this to Charlie, it was all very confusing for him to be able to interpret how if he was playing at school with them then why couldn't he bring it home, even more confusing for him was that on certain days they could bring school reading books home, try as we might to explain to him that that was classed as homework he just couldn't or wouldn't grasp it.

My husband and I gave him the talk on how he shouldn't do it and that his teacher had been right to tell me. Soon after, I was called into school again at the end of the day. This time, it was because Charlie didn't want to stand in line. When they were getting ready to go to lunch, he would push the other children and try to stand away from them. If that didn't work, he could no longer contain his anger and had whacked another little lad around the head with his lunch box. This made the boy cry, and inevitably, his mother would not be happy. I thanked the teacher for letting me know and assured her that we would yet again be having a stern few words when we got home. I felt totally at a loss of what to do or how to handle this situation as I knew full well why Charlie had reacted the way he did because he could not abide anyone being too close to him in whatever circumstance, he didn't even like or want cuddles from my husband or me or anyone! He would wiggle and squirm away from us which is totally devastating and goes against every maternal bone in my body as it is the first thing that you want to do to your child or anyone you love when you see that they are sad or hurt.

At the same time I understood why the teacher wanted us to reassure her that this behaviour would stop, we did have the talk and again, and we took away his favourite toy and sent him to his room, all the usual consequences that you would normally hand out, but this method proved fruitless and apart from continuous crying and screaming for hours on end, and that is no exaggeration it was literally hours! It had no other impact whatsoever, by now I was very tearful and feeling so worried I was taking all of Charlie's quirks and his behaviour very personally and felt that the teachers were blaming my parenting, which that wasn't actually said to me, but it didn't need to be, I could just feel it.

I took Charlie back to our doctor and explained everything to him: how he rarely talked, how he was subdued one minute, and then the next, he would express himself very aggressively. He always went a deathly pale colour if he was under any form of stress, and had even been sick on several occasions. The GP nodded sympathetically and said, unfortunately, as he was still only four, he couldn't refer him to CAMHS (child and mental health service) until Charlie was six. This was because they could say at four, he was acting like a typical child of that age! So I had to wait until he was six to take him back. I knew that all kids play up and are naughty at times, and that's perfectly normal, but I knew this was a lot more than that.

I knew he had autism, and I also knew I was in for a long two years. The next couple of years passed in a blur of reprimands, crying, fighting and an overwhelming feeling of helplessness between us all. It was like Groundhog Day most days; Charlie would say that he was being bullied, or the boys were pushing him around, coming home covered in mud and lots of bruises. Whenever I mentioned it to the teacher, she always said the same, "we have no evidence of this." Well, they wouldn't, as it always happened at lunchtime when they were largely unsupervised by any teachers and only had two dinner ladies who couldn't possibly watch them all at once. I wasn't one of those mums who went to school at the slightest whim; in fact, I only ever went in when things got really bad as I didn't want to be a nuisance; that is where I blame myself partly as I have learned over the years that those who shout the loudest get heard, but back then that wasn't my way, I wanted to work with the school and keep things nice.

So, it carried on back and forth back and forth, as there was so little communication, it was suggested that a homeschool book was to be implemented where I would write any concerns about home or school and vice versa. . . well, that was the plan! It was rarely filled in on the school's part, and it was even rarer that they even read it, as none of my concerns were answered. In the end, the home school book disappeared altogether and wasn't even missed by the school. All I kept getting from the teachers was, "he is fine; boys will be boys. Don't worry," so why do I keep getting called in for his behaviour? That surely isn't right. I just wanted that next year over so I could get Charlie referred and know what we were dealing with, so I could gain the knowledge of what to do to help my poor boy. The time dragged by and at last he was six, and we got referred, the referral took another six months to come through, we went to our first visit to CAMHS which was the first of many many visits.

The lady who we saw was so lovely and kind and I warmed to her straight away, she asked so many questions and made so many notes over the course of our visits, we didn't mind at all as we knew how important this was to get the correct diagnosis. After almost a year and a half that day finally arrived, a lovely consultant sat us all down and present us with her findings which were ASD(autistic spectrum disorder)Asperger with co morbid anxiety along with selective mutism and PDA(pathological demand avoidance)which he fits the profile for, although at the time our CAMHS did not diagnose PDA.

So what with his earlier diagnosis of hypermobility he had a lot going on for a young boy, as well as all of this he had also developed a skin condition called polymorphic light eruption, which is a reaction caused by any sudden changes in heat or sunlight which in turn made his ears, arms and legs swell and go bright red and itch. Even sitting under our lounge lamp would set it off; no wonder he got cross. We felt sad at the time of Charlie's diagnosis of autism, as we were fearful of what his future would be. Still, more than anything, we felt pleased to finally have some answers as to why Charlie had been acting how he had been; with all of his sensory and behavioural issues, it must have been torture for him.

We desperately wanted to help him lead a more comfortable life. I read books and papers on the condition. I learnt that every autistic person is different, just as we all are; I also learnt that what Charlie was expressing was also part and parcel of the autism and that he became frustrated when he didn't feel in control of situations. It wasn't me being a rubbish mum, although, at times, I felt that I was. Thank goodness I had my lovely, caring husband, as we were always there for each other. We explained to Joseph, my mum and other close family and friends about the consultant's findings, and then I went into school and explained the same to his teacher, which I felt fell on deaf ears as she looked at me like I had suddenly grown two heads! I asked her what was wrong, and her reply was," I am so surprised as he is fine in school' little did I know it then, but those few words I was to hear a lot more of in the future!

CAMHS had arranged for a wonderful mental health nurse to work with Charlie both at home and in school to try and make things a bit easier for Charlie and to help teach him different methods to help calm him down and to calm his nerves, the help was going to be for around two months' worth, so I was very hopeful that this would make for an easier path for Charlie, the nurse and I used to have a quick update with each other after each session to see how things were going, it was during one of these updates where she first expressed some concerns she had about the school and if they had taken on board what she had been advising them, we kept on persevering, and I was trying to work with the school, but they just did not get it, for example Charlies class were having a Victorian themed day which meant that they had to re-enact what a typical school day would have been like back in that era.

Charlie is left-handed and so his teacher thought that it would be a great idea to make him use his right hand that day, hard enough for anyone and I understood her logic somewhat as that is what the action would have been back then, but the next part is just plain cruel, as Charlie found it so incredibly difficult to use his right hand he kept forgetting and referred back to his left hand, so his teacher then made him stand in the corner facing the wall and if that wasn't bad enough she then put a dunce hat on his head, of course the whole class found all of this hilarious and erupted into giggles, Charlie came home understandably so distraught and was extremely sad, horrible to see your child in that state especially when it could have easily been avoided. His nurse and I both spoke to the teacher, and her response was, "It wasn't for long." She just did not get autism at all, and I felt my shoulders sag in disappointment and despair.

The nurse and consultant arranged for my husband, me, the headmistress and his class teacher to have a meeting in school. It was to be about explaining traits and reactions of autism and its effects. We all sat around a table in the head's office, and I had never felt as embarrassed as I did when I was in that meeting. The headmistress totally dismissed what the consultant was saying, adding that she didn't feel Charlie was autistic as she had seen no evidence at all of it in school, stating he was very polite and helpful, just a very quiet boy.

Charlie was helpful, kind, caring and polite, but that didn't mean that he didn't have autism." What about all the times I've been called in?" I asked. The homeschool book had disappeared altogether, yet still, she denied it, going bright red in the face during the protests. I became very tearful again; it felt like I was going mad. In the end, the consultant got very stern, coming to the point of explaining that she had worked extremely hard to become a consultant and that they don't diagnose on a whim, so do not undermine my diagnosis. At that moment, I wanted to jump up and kiss the lovely doctor and take her home with me so she could always fight our corner.

It was then arranged through CAMHS that a specialist autism advisory teacher would come into school to help and give advice to the teachers on what autism was and how it could present itself. That happened soon after the meeting, and an absolutely wonderful man called Richard came into school. He was very well known all over the local area. He was extremely good at what he did, somewhat of an expert in the field, and used to give talks all over the place. He suggested that he thought it would be useful if he could give a very short and sweet chat to Charlie's classmates about how they could understand and possibly help Charlie. This idea was soon squashed down. Why oh why was everything so hard, and why didn't she want to help? Meanwhile, Richard said that he would keep in touch and visit the next term again; if I wanted any information, I was to ring him, and he would help me; he said the headmistress had his number, and I was to ask her for it. I left it for a few days and then went to the head and politely asked for Richard's phone number. I explained that he had asked me to get it from her, to which she said, "No, I am not at liberty to give out phone numbers." I replied, "I get that totally, still trying to appease her; after all, it would be a work number and not his private one, still a firm no. What on earth is wrong with this school? Why won't they help us?

When I collected Charlie from school a couple of weeks later, he produced a letter about an upcoming trip to a local wildlife park along with the permission slip and payment slip. The teachers were also after six or seven parents to go along and help supervise the day out. We would all travel together on a coach that was to be hired for the day. "Would you like to go?" I asked Charlie. He nodded eagerly, pointed at me and said, "If you can come, mum." I made sure the next morning we left a bit earlier, so I could put my name down on the list for volunteers, as I knew if I didn't go, then Charlie wouldn't go either. I wrote my name down and double-checked with the teacher to make sure it would be ok, and she said, "Yes, that's great you are coming." So, I felt confident thinking all was sorted. I returned the permission slip and payment promptly. We were both really looking forward to the day out, as it was such a rarity that we went out. It was so nice that Charlie wanted to go, and he absolutely adored animals. The morning of the trip arrived, and all of us helpers met outside the school, waiting for the children to register so we could all get on the coach and be on our way. Then, the headmistress appeared and beckoned me over and abruptly told me that there had been a change of plan and that I could no longer go, as she had already promised another mum a place but had not written it down on the original list.

Well, usually, I am a reasonably calm person, but almost immediately, I could feel a wave of pure pricking anger wash over me; it was almost as if my arms and legs had gone numb. How much more awkward could this woman be? It was like she was goading me. With exasperated tears in my eyes, I just about managed to say, "You know he wouldn't want to go if I didn't come along; I thought that was the understanding." maybe that was her plan all along... who knows." It will do him good to go without you, it will give him more independence and confidence" this remark bemused me as according to her he had no issues with confidence, she was totally contradicting herself. Yet again, I bowed down and said that I would ask Charlie if he would go without me. I knew full well what his answer would be, but sometimes you have to jump through hoops to prove a point, something that I was going to get very good at as time went on, unfortunately. Lo and behold, Charlie's answer was indeed no. The head was not happy and got cross with Charlie for not being a big, brave boy! Those are her words exactly. It was more than apparent now that 'the talk by the CAMHS team had absolutely had no impression on her whatsoever, or maybe it did, but she was choosing to ignore the advice. I sound paranoid, I know, but that is how she was making me feel.

"Right! I shall take Charlie home, and I would like a full refund of my money." Charlie was beside himself with disappointment, and the look on his face spoke volumes and one I shall never forget. I found my inner strength from somewhere, and between a mixture of anger towards her and sheer sadness for my son, I said in the strongest voice that I could muster that I was going to be speaking to someone about this. I had no idea at that time who that person might be, but I just had to say something to release at least some of my feelings. It might seem what I said was mild, and yes, it probably was, but again, it had been instilled in me from a very young age that you do not make a fuss about things and that you have respect for teachers, doctors and anyone who was a professional. So, you see, it was going against the grain to speak out like this. In the end, after what seemed an age, she eventually relented and let me go along with Charlie on the trip… I even thanked her, which, looking back now, makes me cringe. Although it was a lovely day trip, the occasion was soured for me; Charlie really enjoyed himself, which was the most important thing. He even went a little way ahead of me with his classmates to look at the animals. He was still on the outside edge of the group, but at least he wanted to venture off, even if it was just for a little while

When Charlie was around seven, I joined a local support group called POSCH (parents of special children). It was a really nice, welcoming atmosphere and a good bunch of mums. A right mixed bag of characters who all had different characters and came from all walks of life, but we all had one thing in common, which bonded us together. The group was once a fortnight and I really looked forward to those Monday mornings, around once a month the ladies that ran the group used to invite a specialist in to talk to us, and we had a chance at the end to ask any questions that we may have had. A lot of the mums made good use of this time and had lots of questions to ask.

I also had lots of questions in my head that I wanted to ask and that's just where they stayed in my head, me being me I just didn't have enough confidence in me anymore to speak up, I so wish I had, but it was still good to listen. Everyone's plight and journey is different from each other's, but I can remember thinking about the more braver ones in the group, at least yours. child goes to school as by this time it was getting more and more difficult to get him out of his bedroom and even harder to get him to want to go to school, whilst I felt empathy for the other mums and really admired how they coped, it seemed some of their children were very disruptive, would often upturn tables and chairs, shout and swear at the teachers, these children seemed to get the help they so needed whereas Charlie presented as a very quiet shy polite boy in school, so in turn, was forgotten about and left to his own devices, at least that's how it felt to me. Disruptive children meant that other children would complain to their parents, and in turn, the parents would complain to the school, which would mean they would get help. My kind-hearted boy didn't get believed in, let alone helped! It all seemed very unfair.

He was so withdrawn at school, and it was only when he was at home that he would explode with the most awful outbursts and rages. His face would go bright red, and his head would throb. It was like walking on eggshells as the slightest thing would trigger a rage, even something simple, like asking what he would like for tea. His brain was just so stressed that he couldn't cope; they call this the bottle of pop effect, where they bottle up the stress all day at school, and then when they get home, they feel safe and secure so they can let the lid off resulting in a big explosion. Imagine trying to deal with that all day, every day.

One of the final straws came one afternoon, just after lunch. I was due to go to school and help supervise the children on a walk

34

to the village allotment, where the school had a small plot. When I went over and waited in the classroom for registration to begin, I looked around and looked around again and asked, "Where is my son?" The teacher looked around and called his name, but it was very apparent that Charlie was not in class. I ran out and shouted his name; I had an ice-cold chill washing over me. I ran, still calling out his name in the playground, and then I saw him backed up against a wall by a member of staff. They were both red in the face. I asked, "What's happened?" The reply was, "He has been a very naughty boy. He kicked and punched another child." I was once again crestfallen to hear this and looked at Charlie and I just shook my head.

We had told Charlie if he could feel himself getting agitated then he must try to take himself out for a time-out until the feeling passed, easier said than done, and it obviously had not worked on this occasion. It was a scorching hot summer day, and with a combination of the heat and all the upset, Charlie was very suddenly sick. I took him home, as he was in no fit state at that point, to go walking to the allotment. Once at home, I helped him calm down with some cold flannels and gave him the space that he needed on his own. It was only later on, once he was calmer, that I asked him what had made him react in such a way. He explained that they were playing football on the field, and one of the boys had tackled Charlie hard, so he had pushed the other lad over. Reading between the lines, I felt that the other boy hadn't meant any malice toward Charlie and was indeed doing a tackle, and that Charlie had misinterpreted it with his literal way of thinking and stickler for rules. It had all been blown out of proportion; Charlie didn't see it that way at all, as another trait of autism is finding it very difficult to reason with people.

We had a chat, or rather, I did all of the chatting while Charlie was nodding his head in agreement. I had more or less put it out of my mind until later that evening when my friend rang me who had a daughter in the same class as Charlie. She asked me if Charlie was ok. I replied, "He is now. Why?" She then went on to explain that she was trying to settle her daughter for bed, but she was very upset over what she had seen at lunchtime earlier that day. "What did she see?" I almost didn't want to hear what it was, as my friend would only ring over something like this if it were serious. Her daughter had seen Charlie kick and push the other child over onto the grass, but what she had told her mum she had seen next was just almost unbelievable.

She went on to say that just after the incident, a member of staff (the same staff member I had seen with Charlie at lunch) went over to Charlie, pushed him to the ground, and shouted at him, "See? Not nice, is it Charlie? To be pushed." I felt sick to my stomach, and then the red-hot anger came over me. I was shaking from head to toe with rage, disbelief, and sadness for my poor son. Later that evening, once I had spoken to my husband about what had gone on, who was equally annoyed and upset, I helped Charlie into the bath, and that's when I noticed a small bruise on his. I didn't want to put words into his mouth, so I very casually asked the usual questions about what his day had been like... and how lunchtime play had been. Straight away, he said, "That horrible lady pushed me over, and everyone laughed." I was beyond mad and did not sleep a wink that night, waiting for the morning to come, so I could get to the bottom of this latest incident.

I was still raging come 9 am and made my way straight to Charlie's classroom to report what I had been told. I kept as calm as I could. I did not shout and wasn't rude. I tried to stay composed and had tears threatening to spill over my bottom lids. My face was pulsing with emotion. I told the teacher, and she said that I needed to go and report it immediately to the headmistress, so off I went with as much gusto as I could muster and told her everything. She didn't believe me, I could tell instantly, but she

36

did say that she would speak to the member of staff and get back to me. I told her that I would be back by 3 pm for a full explanation.

When I went back over later, the head was waiting for me with an expression that I was not used to seeing, which was a mixture of guilt and a smile! She took me into her office and offered, "Tea or coffee, Mrs. Peacock?" Now, I knew something was definitely wrong. The member of staff had admitted what she had done to my son and was seemingly very apologetic. The decision was left in my courts as to whether or not we wanted to take it further. I didn't really want it to cost her her job as she had been in the past fairly decent, but nevertheless, she had overstepped the mark. The head reassured me that she would report it to the appropriate channels. Two days later, I asked if she had reported the incident, to which she said that she had and that they were happy if I was to let the headmistress deal with it internally. I stupidly agreed but stated that I didn't want that woman anywhere near my son ever again. My son never did get that apology, and looking back now, I strongly believe that my complaint only made it as far as the head's office where it was left under the carpet.

The next term, Charlie was due to start swimming lessons every other Thursday, which pleased him as he still liked the feel of water. Although he couldn't yet swim, he enjoyed the warmth and calmness that water gave him. So, armed with his goggles, bathing hat, and swim trunks, he was all set to go. He went to school looking forward to swimming; he would be going on the coach just after lunch to the local swimming pool. The parents were encouraged to go and watch from the viewing point upstairs, which overlooked the pool. It was nice upstairs as there was a small café where you could buy tea or coffee and a slice of cake, which of course we mums did. We would take it to one of the tables and settle down to watch our children enjoying the water, and of course, it was lovely to have a natter and catch up with the other mums. Charlie was having a great time splashing in the water, and it was so lovely to see his happy little face. I was keen for Charlie to learn to swim, so I was pleased that this first play session had gone well. All of us mums arrived back at school to await the arrival of the coach. As it was near home time, we could wait and then take them straight home. The coach seemed very late coming back, and I wondered why; it was the same the following week, and I soon found out why! Charlie was taking an age to dry and dress himself, and it was holding the whole class. He had to put talc on so that he didn't feel sticky and had to be absolutely dry before anything else could happen; it had all to do with his sensory processing.

Along with this, he had to apply his cream for his allergies as well, so I can well imagine the frustration that this would have caused. It really could take forever. It took him long enough with me helping him at home, let alone him trying to do it on his own. It was apparent that this was causing problems, and once again, Charlie was made to feel different, so much so that he didn't want to go swimming anymore and had to stay behind at school with the younger children. It really was one thing after another, and I was getting at my wit's end with it all. Nothing was improving at all; in fact, it was getting worse, so much so that Charlie was now totally refusing to go to school or even get out of bed, something drastic had to be done.

Several other parents had taken their children out of school for one reason or another. I really didn't want to go down that route of changing schools at this late stage in primary school, as by now he was coming to the end of year four. This would mean, once in year five, he only had two more years to go until he would go to the secondary school in the next town. And we wanted him to go up with the few friends that he had managed to make.

If tried to even gently cajole him to get up for school then he would literarily erupt and get very verbally aggressive with me, if

I pushed harder, then he would grab whatever was close to hand and launch at me at the same time swearing at me, this wasn't my dear sweet hearted Charlie I knew that, this was a very scared little boy who wasn't having his needs met at school and the only way he could articulate it was by this response of taking it out on me as he felt safe with me, it didn't make it any easier for me to go through seeing your child in such a rage that you are actually frightened of what he might do next, I was forever walking on eggshells. Some days I could cope better, other days I would end up in uncontrollable sobs on his bedroom floor just praying out loud for someone to help... Please God help, please god help us. It really was that bad, by this time Charlie wasn't coming out of his room at all only to go to the toilet, he was so depressed and down and felt very remorseful after his outburst at me. It was breaking us and day by day a little bit more of me ebbed away, it happened slowly so I hardly noticed at that stage.

I would ring his school every morning to let them know that he wouldn't be in again as he was so anxious and miserable, the reply was always the same, "not a problem Mrs. Peacock, don't you worry". What hope did we have, I didn't know who or where to turn to. His CAMHS appointment had been brought forward but was still a good while away. Several of my friends had given very good reports on a primary school in Bicester, so grabbing the bull by the horns I rang and made an appointment to have a look around. Straight away we got such a lovely feeling from the moment you walked through the doors, a receptionist met Kenny and me. She had the most amazing warm and genuine smile it put both of us at ease.

Once we had looked around and asked if they could accommodate Charlie, which they could, we then managed to get Charlie in to have a look, after all, it was one thing us liking it but it would be Charlie who had to feel comfortable with the choice, as it went, he liked it to... but they were full and had no spaces left, not a surprise really as it really was a lovely nurturing school. We really wanted Charlie to get a place so as he could have the chance of at least two years of education and more importantly happiness before the next stage.

Now what? I wondered. Coincidently, during this time, through my support group, I had managed to access a lady called a home school link worker. So, I rang her to see if she had any ideas and arranged to come to our home and have a chat, what a lovely person she was, very understanding but also very practical and that is just what we needed, so with her help, we appealed the decision which entailed lots of paperwork and I had to gather as much evidence as I could to fight our case as you had to prove that the preferred school would be the best school in the area for our son.

It was all so long-drawn and time-consuming, but it would all be worth it if we were successful. The homeschool link lady was so helpful, and I wouldn't have been able to do it without her. This gave us a small slither of hope after all the awful days, which had now gone on for well over a year. We dared not get too hopeful, but the next day, I set the wheels in motion with the appeals team and posted the big bundle of paperwork; now, the only thing we could do was wait.

In around five weeks or so, we received a letter calling Kenny and me to the appeals panel meeting in the county hall in Oxford. It had been explained to me that a panel of around six people of various professions, not linked to any of the schools so as they could remain independent, would ask me lots of questions and want as much information as possible. I was extremely nervous and was shaking even before we got in the car, but armed with my folder, I was determined to fight my son's corner, and this was my one and only chance to put his case across. We had already decided that I would do most of the talking, which I found very daunting as I am fairly quiet, but my husband is even quieter and gets very emotional when he talks about our son.

We arrived and didn't have to wait long until we were both called in. We had to sit facing the six appeals people, and it was a huge long table in quite an old-fashioned dark room. I was asked to stand once all of the introductions were done. I don't know how I stood, as by this time, my legs were almost to jelly; I stood and looked at the six stern faces. I knew that they had to act very professionally. It was now or never. I had to fight, and fight, I did. I spoke from my heart and hardly had to revert to my notes. I cried as well; I just couldn't help it, and I told them everything. It just all came out. I must have looked an awful sight as I had cried so much my eyes were so swollen to the point of almost shutting; seeing me so upset made my lovely, caring husband cry too; he tried to hold them back but just couldn't.

The one that seemed to be in charge or lead the panel was an elderly gentleman who had these little round glasses that just perched on the bridge of his nose. He smiled kindly at me and said that I could now sit down, and then thanked me. I was very relieved to sit down, as my legs were now as heavy as lead. I scanned all six faces to see if I could read anything from their expressions, but they were well-practiced, and all had poker faces. They asked if we could take a seat outside the room and that they would call us in presently.

We didn't have to wait too long before they called us back in. They had reached a decision and had all agreed, and we would receive it in writing in the next day or so. I wanted to ask them to give me a clue but thought better of it. I remember it was a Friday, and I was thinking that this weekend was going to drag by, and it did! Come Monday morning, I was up earlier than usual, waiting for the post. When the post came, the letter was there. I stared at it for a good while, almost too afraid to open it. I looked at the contents with one eye shut; I scanned the letter until I got to the words. We had been successful in our appeal and won! Yes! Charlie was going to get his new start!

CHAPTER FIVE

It had been decided that Charlie would start his new school in September after the summer holidays, as it would be a new term and a new start for him. We had a whole six weeks to help prepare him. We even managed to get Charlie to come shopping with us for his new uniform so he could pick out what lunch box he would like and, of course, the new school shoes. Which always caused great stress and took hours of searching for the right ones. They had to feel just right in the sense that no knots could be felt over the socks, the tongue had to lay perfectly flat and absolutely no touching the sides of his ankles. So, you can just imagine that task was near on impossible. Nevertheless, we had to stay as calm as humanly possible and smile through very often gritted teeth. If he sensed that we were rushing him or getting a bit impatient, then that would be the end of the shopping trip. We would have to all face it again another day!

I always liked it when the school holidays came around, as it was a much-needed break for us all, no more stressing every day at the prospect that will he go or will he not go to school. I knew he wouldn't, but every day, I tried regardless. We decided to have a week away at the coast, it was a quaint village called Scratby on the Norfolk coast. We went to the same place every year as it was so nice and friendly with a really old-fashioned seaside holiday feel. Both boys loved it so much that they would both pack their little cases a week or so in advance. As long as Charlie could pack his favourite teddies, cars and stones, then it would be the one week of the year that we could guarantee would happen so, in turn, look forward to something. Both boys loved the beach and the sea.

Charlie was especially drawn to the sea and hunting for more unusual stones and shells. Another firm favourite was the two penny machines in the arcade. All year, my thoughtful, kind-hearted Mum would save all her pennies up in two empty ice cream tubs. They would both sit on the living room floor, sharing the money that had already been counted and shared by my Mum. Still, just to make sure, Charlie would want to go through both tubs again, and believe me, Charlie would know if it was one coin out. He has such a sharp eye for detail.

On the morning of our adventure, we would set off at around six in the morning so as to get there nice and early. It took roughly three hours to get to Scratby, and we would stop off at the services for the usual toilet break and then eat some sandwiches that I had made for the journey. It was all part of the adventure. We always used to stay in a little chalet on a holiday park, but as the boys grew, inevitably, the chalet became too small for us all, so we then would rent a lovely good-sized bungalow for the week. It was situated in the most beautiful spot, overlooking the wide expanse of the sea. If you walked just over some grassland and down the sand dunes, you were on the beach. It was just idyllic, weather permitting, of course, as the Norfolk coast can be very brisk even on a summer's day; sometimes, if it did rain, it was nice and cosy just to have a day in and play board games and look out over at the rough sea.

It was a fairly small village that stretched along the coastline. It had more or less everything you could possibly want, a launderette, village store, gift shops, a bakery that sold the most amazing bread and doughnuts, and you could not help to not be tempted as the smell was out of this world. But by far on top of the list was the fish and chip shop and the two-penny arcade, just as you would imagine it would be for two excited boys! Great Yarmouth was only a few miles away, so we would often visit and go to the fun fair or have a ride down the prom on the horse-drawn carriage. Another day, we would hire a small boat and explore the Norfolk broads, which we all thoroughly enjoyed. As long as we got back to the bungalow in the afternoon, so Charlie could have his downtime alone in his bedroom, all was calm.

We would still have a couple of meltdowns, and we knew the signs to try and avoid one; it was very difficult for Joseph to understand, so very often, either myself or Kenny would have alone time with Joe and share our time between them, which worked well. The evenings would be so nice, as we were on holiday I didn't really want to be cooking all the time. So, for a couple of nights, Kenny and Joseph would do a BBQ, and another night we would go to the local restaurant, which was such a treat for us all. We often get a takeaway on the way back from the penny machines.

On the very last night, it had become a family tradition that on the very last night, we would eat fish and chips on the beach and watch the boats and ships all lit up in the ocean; that was our all-time favourite meal, as I don't think you can beat fish and chips eaten outside they always seem to taste so much nicer, especially on the beach. Our last night was always sad for the boys, and they would get a bit teary. We were sad as well, as we knew all too soon that we would have to return to reality and what we had all been struggling with and going through for so long. However, on this occasion, I felt more hopeful than I had in a long time, as Charlie was going to start at his new school and enter a new chapter in his life. The rest of the summer holidays went by, and the nearer September was approaching, the more anxious Charlie was becoming. I could sense that all too familiar gnaw in my stomach; his smiley, cheeky little face had once again gone and had been replaced by a pale face of worry.

He was having headaches daily and was so exhausted that he would take two hours of sleep in the afternoon. The cause, as I knew only too well, was anxiety; he barely left his bedroom, and if I tried to encourage him, he would become very verbally aggressive towards me, shouting, swearing and calling me the most hurtful names. It made me so sad to see Charlie like this, as this was not the real him. I was beginning to wonder if we would ever see the old Charlie again. It wasn't that long ago, or so it seemed, that if he was having a good day and felt able to come downstairs, I would make us all a huge bowl of popcorn and open some crisps, draw the curtains, and my two boys would snuggle into me chomping on the treats watching a movie or two or playing bowling on the Wii. Nowadays, it would just be Joe and me, which was still nice. Still, of course, I was well aware of Charlie isolating himself upstairs, which was utterly heartbreaking. I had started to get a nagging doubt in the pit of my stomach that he was not going to be able to attend his new school. The wave of dread was washing over me the nearer and nearer the time got. I tried to put it out of my mind and think positively, I really did, but deep down, I knew.

The plan was that Charlie and I would get the bus from our village to school, and luckily, there was a bus stop directly outside of the school. Once I had dropped Charlie off, I would then walk the two miles back to the village and then at the end of the day, I would walk back in, and then both of us would get the bus home. I don't drive, so walking was my only option. I didn't mind as I liked walking and found it cleared my head and enabled me to think, but even if I had hated walking, I would have walked to the ends of the earth to make my child happy and content. That was the plan!...

That first morning, I very gently but confidently woke Charlie up at 7 am, as he had requested. Cautiously, I said, "Time to wake up, Charlie," gently touching his shoulder at the same time. There was no response from Charlie, so I repeated what I had said minutes before. Charlie then yelled at me "I know what the time is as I heard you the first time" at the top of his voice. I kept calm and understood that it wasn't him being mean to me, it was his anxiety; nevertheless, it still stung. I made some breakfast for us all to give him time to come to, after which I asked Charlie to please go and have a wash and clean to clean his teeth. "No!" was his reply in a flat, deadpan tone. After much talking and coaxing from both Kenny and myself, we finally managed to get Charlie dressed. His sensory issues were through the roof; if his sweater had come off once, it must have come off ten more times as he was insisting that it didn't feel right and that the label was prickling him. I knew that there was nothing left of the label as the day before I had spent trimming to nothing. Once the sweater was comfy, it was then his socks and then the shoes, and then his collar. I was staying very calm and patient with him as I didn't want to antagonise him as then we would have had no chance of getting him to school; it really was like walking on eggshells. I didn't want us missing our bus either, especially on the first morning and all of this was stacking up in me. I was feeling very hot and panicky inside. Kenny had said not to worry as he could drive us both to school as he had taken a couple of days off of work to help us. I really didn't want to accept the lift as I wanted to start as we were meant to carry on, and I didn't want Charlie wanting his dad to take him in the car every morning, as that would not be possible due to work.

The time had raced on by, and I was more than aware that the bus would not be an option this morning, so off we all went in the car. My shoulders sagged with relief when we arrived at the school as I felt that was the hardest part for Charlie and that now that he was here, the teachers would help make him feel less anxious, which they did, and they were all so kind. They led him away from us both. It had been arranged that I would collect him at lunchtime on that first day, as he would be exhausted from having not been in school for so long. When I collected him at lunch, he looked so pale and ill. He complained of having a splitting headache. The kind teacher smiled and said that he had been fine in school. Charlie nodded in agreement when asked if he had had a nice time. We said goodbye to the teacher, with me saying an encouraging

"See you in the morning." As we got nearer to the car, poor Charlie was promptly sick on the pavement. I tried to help him wipe himself down with some wet wipes, but he pushed me away and had a resentful look on his face once we had got semi-clean. We were on our way home I asked, "Did you have a nice time?" He shrugged his shoulders, and it was clear he didn't want to talk, which was fine and understandable, so I left any more questions for another time.

Later on that day, I asked him if he had been able to tell his teacher about his headache; he hadn't been able to, as he said he couldn't talk at all. I had made him, in preparation for this transition, some communication cards with words written on them; examples would be, I want the toilet, I feel sick, or I need time out, please. That sort of thing was an alternative to talking, but my poor, sweet, sensitive boy had just been too frozen with overwhelming emotion to even show the cards, let alone put his hand up. We still kept positive for the next day as, after all, this was only the first day and was bound to be nerve-wracking for him; tomorrow is another day which will be much easier for you, Charlie. I told him with confidence that did not meet my feelings inside.

The next morning wasn't any different. In fact, it was much, much worse; the day had started much the same as the previous day with exactly the same planned routine that Charlie liked; the difference this morning, though, was that Charlie didn't get out of bed or eat breakfast or wash and dress. Instead he buried his head under the covers and was gripping tightly to the duvet so we could not get to him easily to help him dress. Now, I knew only too well what this meant, and it was history repeating itself in all its glory. I tried to take hold of the duvet, but it ended up being a tug of war, and I wasn't winning. Kenny came to try and help me, and he is so good with both boys and just knows what to say at the right time and is very calming in stressful situations. So, with his reasoning

47

skills, I was still hopeful of getting Charlie into school; however, unfortunately, this time, even Kenny couldn't work his magic. We did manage to pull the duvet off of Charlie and sit him on the edge of his bed, where we started to attempt to dress him, something that we had done on several occasions in the past. Now, however, Charlie was much taller and stronger. I'm only 4 feet and 11 inches, weighing 7 ½ stones, whereas Charlie was nearly 10 years old, being much taller and heavier than me. We had just about dressed his top half, which had gone well. Charlie cooperated and let us help him. When I went to put his trousers on, he went rigid and stiff as a board. I then tried to put his socks and shoes on, which was just impossible as he was twisting and scrunching his toes up in a ball. It was a battle of wills, and we were all getting agitated and looking red in the face. My back was killing me from the bending over and all the struggling. Then, at exactly the same time, both Kenny and I looked at each other and said, "Enough! No more! This is making him worse." I slumped to the floor with exhaustion but mainly with sorrow for Charlie.

We desperately needed professional help, but no one was listening, let alone helping. I felt such a failure as a mother and a total letdown to everyone, especially as I had fought tooth and nail to get him into this lovely school. I cried and cried, holding my temples, which were, by this time, throbbing with pain. I just couldn't help crying; I was so desperate by now. I knew I had to try and compose myself to make that phone call that I was so used to doing and naively thought that I wouldn't be doing again; firstly I settled Charlie by way of letting him calm down on his own with a glass of water, then I calmed myself as much as I could and rang the school. The secretary was so understanding and kind, and I always had that same response every time I rang. Every morning was the same. I tried and tried to persuade Charlie to go, but it was fruitless, making us both very stressed. The school sent over a video for Charlie that showed his teachers and his would-be classmates, and each one said, "Hello, Charlie, we are looking forward to seeing you soon." They had filmed his empty page with his name marked above it, all ready and waiting for his return. That really got to me as it was such a stark visual reminder of what he was missing out on. With all the other pages full, there was an obvious gaping space where his book bag and coat should have been. It was such a lovely, kind, and thoughtful gesture from the school.

They really wanted Charlie there, but I knew it was going to take more than this wonderful video to achieve that. I kept seeing in my mind's eye that empty page, and I sobbed and sobbed from the very pit of my stomach; anything would set me off crying lately. I would stand alone looking out of my front window and watching neighbours' children happily going to school with their mothers, or the older children going to school together, sharing a joke or two and doing what children are supposed to do and having fun. Poor Charlie must have felt so low, and as his mother, I couldn't help him in any way apart from showing him love and kindness. The few friends he had made at primary school had long moved on as kids do. Charlie was all alone with zero confidence, which had now developed into a school phobia. Why oh why didn't his old headmistress listen to the advice from the professionals, and why oh why hadn't I stood up for him more and fought his corner more? It did not come easily for me to speak out. It wasn't in my nature then (it is now!) I had always been taught just to accept things and that people in authority know best. The other part was fear if I had said anything, she would have made his situation worse if that was possible. I had seen it myself with other mothers.

I was feeling weak, pathetic, and so desperate. Please, just somebody, anybody, help us! I would sob out loud. I asked our GP to refer Charlie back to CAMHS, and after being put on a very long waiting list, he was finally seen by a child psychologist who suggested medication to help Charlie cope better with his by now crippling anxiety. We really didn't want to go down the medication route, but when Charlie himself expressed that he would like to try it, we all agreed that was the way to go. So, here we were, our 10-year-old boy was prescribed Prozac; it had no effect at all. So, after a few weeks, the dosage was increased. It did help somewhat, but nowhere near enough to help ease him back into school. By now, it was March 2013, and still, no school or education was being accessed, so CAMHS spoke to the school. Kenny and I said that they could refer Charlie to the Oxfordshire Hospital school education team. It was explained that their role would be initially for a teacher from the hospital school to visit Charlie at home for six sessions so as to build up trust and, hopefully, a rapport. After the six sessions at home, if successful, then it would progress to a further six sessions at the early intervention hub in the next town. Following that, the final stage would be the teacher would reintroduce Charlie back into school for the remainder of the last six sessions, so in theory, after twelve weeks, he would be back in school and on the right way. This came as very welcome news and sounded just what Charlie needed, and along with his medication, I thought we had all finally got a much-needed breakthrough; Charlie was so pleased as well, as he really wanted to be in school. So, with renewed optimism, we all had new hope, and it eased the pressure enormously. It all took a good few weeks to arrange, as these things always do.

It was May 2013 when there was a knock on the door, one we had been expecting as it was the first day that the lady from hospital schools was due to visit. I opened the door with a warm, welcoming smile and a friendly, "Hello, nice to meet you." A very stoney-faced, strict-looking lady met my eye and said a simple, short, and curt "Hello." My stomach just dropped to my feet. I had a bad feeling immediately about this, but thought, "No, Sharon, fate couldn't be that cruel, could it?" I dismissed my feelings and kept things positive. "Would you like tea or coffee?" I offered.

Her reply was, "Yes, I will have coffee but no milk, as I'm allergic and will go into anaphylactic shock."

"Oh, blimey," I said, making a mental note, never ever to get any milk near her at any time! "How awful for you," I sympathised.

"Yes, it is. I have to carry an EpiPen in my bag just in case".

I invited her into the living room and introduced her to Charlie. I had already set a board game up for them on the dining room table, and once they had begun to play. She started talking to Charlie, "You know, Charlie, all children must go to school." I heard her say; Charlie nodded his head in agreement. Her remark pricked me a bit as it made me think that she thought that I hadn't tried hard enough, but I kept quiet and said nothing. She then went on to talk briefly about anxiety, producing out of her trouser pocket a rose-coloured crystal. As she showed it to Charlie, she explained that she gets anxious and that the crystal really helped her, and asked why doesn't Charlie try it as well. I remember thinking to myself, "Oh well. That's it then, the answer to all our prayers!" Now, while I do believe somewhat in alternative and holistic therapies, I knew that it was going to take a lot more than some crystal to get Charlie through this. My heart sank just that little bit more when she asked Charlie if he would like Mum to get him one, and of course, he nodded eagerly, especially with his fascination with stones! She then turned to me and went on to say that, in fact, she herself was in the process of coming off of antidepressants and sleeping pills and was having some side effects. "Oh dear," I said, not knowing what else to say. She then went on to ask me if I could see her eye twitching. "No, not that I've noticed," I replied somewhat wearily. She then said in urgency, "Quick, look now, it's doing it now. Can you see it?" I replied, "Well, yes, I can now that you've mentioned it, but I wouldn't have noticed unless you had pointed it out" I tried to reassure her. With that, she carried on playing the game with

Charlie. I thought that it was a bit strange, but I reasoned that I didn't know this woman and maybe it was just her way.

The hour visit was soon over, and she explained that she would be back the following week to take Charlie to the hospital school. Immediately, I could visibly see Charlie tense up. "I thought that you were doing home visits for six weeks first," I quickly said. Her reply made my heart sink even further, "Oh no way, I haven't got time for that." Then she followed up with a laugh and a sarcastic "If only!"

"But I thought that was the understanding of how it worked," I replied.

"No, no, the quicker I can get him into school, the quicker I can get onto the next one."

That's when I thought you were setting Charlie up for a fall, but she had the sort of air about her that you wouldn't dare question her. After all, she was the expert, and I didn't want to appear pushy. My god, do I wish that I had been pushy! But in typical Sharon-style politeness, I kept quiet yet again.

I did say that I didn't think that method would work. So, in the end, very begrudgingly, she agreed to one more home visit but made it very clear that then she would be taking him to the hub. After she left, Charlie said, "I don't like her mum," as he made his way back up to his room. "Me and you both, Charlie." I thought inwardly but, of course, never voiced it to him as this was our lifeline to get him into school, although I was having serious doubts about this, and once again, I felt as flat as a pancake. A voice interrupted my thoughts, and it was coming from upstairs. It was Charlie, "Please, mum, don't let her take me." I reassured him that she knew best and that we would only have to have her for a few weeks. It didn't cut the mustard with young Charlie though!

The next visit came around quickly, and the same procedure unfolded as the week before, only this time, she looked even more strict and had a no-nonsense persona about her. She was a very slim, tallish lady in her fifties, I would guess, and had short cropped blonde hair; she always wore a checked lumberjack style shirt and skinny jeans with Doc Martin style boots. No matter how friendly I was to her, she always made me feel uncomfortable as she still hadn't smiled. Once inside, she asked Charlie if he would like to have a bounce on his trampoline, to which he nodded. Maybe she did have a heart and wasn't so bad after all, I thought. Wrong!

After about ten minutes, Charlie got tired and stopped bouncing and sat cross-legged in the middle of the trampoline, looking at the grass below the netting. Julie, as I will call her, suggested that we should all go for a walk to the village park. "What a good idea," I said, trying to sound upbeat and keen. Charlie promptly shook his head in a firm no action. This did not go down at all well with Julie; it was easy to tell from her stiffened body language and the enormous sigh that came from within her. "Right! Ok then, I and your Mum will go without you. Come on, Mum." She said briskly.

"I can't just leave him on his own out here."

"Yes, you can. You need to show him just because he doesn't want to go doesn't mean that he won't stop you from going."

Fortunately, my Mum was on hand to watch Charlie for me whilst we went out for a walk. We were gone for about an hour and talked about just everything and anything but Charlie. I didn't want to walk and have a chit-chat with her. I wanted her to help me with my son. When we arrived back at my house, she got in her car and left. My Mum said, "That was a strange thing to do."

"Yes, a bit odd," I agreed, "but I guess it's just how she does things." Of course, looking back now, it was indeed a very odd thing to do, in my opinion.

The next week, when she was due to collect us both to go to the hub, my husband was off of work for the day, so between us, we managed to get Charlie into the car and take him, with the promise that I would not leave him. Julie met us at the door of the classroom, and I thought that she would have been pleased to see Charlie. Well, if she was, then she gave nothing away in her expression. We entered the classroom, which had about five other students sitting at tables, who were all much older than Charlie at around sixteen to eighteen years old. They were all studying towards their GCSE exams, the other teacher was a man in his forties and seemed much more friendly, and I thought to myself, trust us to get the grumpy one. Typical!

Now, with both teachers helping the other students, Charlie was given two or three-word searches to do and sat quietly at a table. Then the male teacher did some maths with him, which Charlie enjoyed. I could tell he was happy and eager to please as he sat up straight in his chair and was really trying his hardest to take in what the teacher was explaining to him. It made me both extremely proud and, at the same time, sad to see Charlie so willing and full of hope; he wasn't a naughty, disruptive child. He was just a very worried, scared little boy. We were there for around two hours when the lesson ended for the day, and once outside, I asked if he had liked the hub. He indicated, 'No with a firm shake of his head, closely followed up with, can't see the point of it. If all I am going to do is word search, I can do that at home. Plus, they are all older than me.'

I know, Charlie, but you have to try and give it a good go so that they can see that you are really trying and wanting to go back to school, I reasoned.

I didn't hold out for the next session in a week's time, but I never let Charlie know my thoughts. Still trying to keep an upbeat, positive spin on things.

On the morning of the next visit, I helped Charlie to get ready, and he came downstairs, which is usually a very good sign. Next, he put his socks on but not his shoes… not such a good sign. I gently tried to persuade him to put his shoes on so that he would be all ready. No reply, nothing. I could tell by his body language that he wasn't going to go, and I could physically feel myself starting to shake with worry as I just imagined how cross Julie was going to be. I was dreading it. I have always hated letting people down, and there has to be a darn good reason why I did so. I was not looking forward to the doorbell ringing at nine. Would she be mad at me for thinking that I hadn't bothered even to try? If only she could see the time, effort and patience it took us to get this far in the morning. I was so tired of the mental stress I had a permanent head and backache, let alone how Charlie was feeling.

It was pure torture seeing him so wound up. The doorbell rang at nine sharp, and I walked down our hall to answer it. At that moment, I wished our hall was ten miles long just to delay what her response would be. I opened the door with my normal, bright, and breezy smile and good morning, quickly followed by a wobbling voice that said, "I'm sorry, I'm really struggling with Charlie this morning, and I don't think he will go." Without uttering a single word, she sped by me straight through into the living room and said, "Right, get your shoes on." No good morning smile or nothing; this was not boding well at all; as I thought, Charlie shook his head in that familiar no shake that I had gotten to know.

The next turn of events that happened, I still can't comprehend all of these years later, and I really have struggled to try and work out why she did what she did next. At the time, it all happened so quickly, and still, I thought she was a professional; that's what I thought at the time, and I trusted her judgement and take on things. She picked up my son's leg and was trying to stuff his foot into his trainer, and then he did his usual scrunching up of his toes as I knew only too well that she would have no chance of getting them on; at this point the time I would stop if he were doing that to me as it was achieving nothing except more angst. It was a real battle of wills between them both, and I could see the sheer determination in equal measures on both of their faces.

Julie was getting crosser and redder by the second. I was crying with my hands on either side of my face, not knowing what on earth to do. Next, she turned her back on Charlie so as she was facing away from him. She then bent down and put one of his legs between her own and went on to clamp his leg, so it was wedged between her own. Charlie's remaining leg, which by now was wriggling and kicking like crazy and he was desperately trying to use it to escape. His top half had gone rigid, and he was starting to slide off the sofa, "Please, please stop! Someone is going to get hurt." I heard myself say. Julie's reply was, "Don't you worry, I'm used to this, as I worked in a prison for naughty boys." Just as she turned her head to tell me, Charlie saw his chance and acted on it, "Oh yeah? Take this then, you bitch'' as he attempted to give her a swift kick to the head, but she was very quick to block it and quite gleefully announced, "Nice try, Charlie." Well, that inflamed him even more, "Get off me, you ugly bitch'' he retorted. I was, by this time, nearly hysterical. I had never been in a situation like this before, nor do I ever want to again, "No, no Charlie, please stop. You're making it all even worse and getting her even madder." By this time, I was crying so much I thought I would be sick and couldn't feel my legs at all.

I was a shaking wreck who could not think or see straight, and I was so confused about whether she should even be doing this or not, as I had read a lot about teachers having to do training in restraint, so it must be all above board, didn't it? Charlie managed to wriggle free and ran into the downstairs bathroom and locked himself in. She ran after him, but he was just that bit quicker, much to her annoyance. My god, if I thought she was mad before, she was absolutely fuming now; she wanted me to ring my husband and get him home from work as she didn't want to be alone with Charlie in that state," ironic that it was her that had got him in that state in the first place. I explained that there was no way I was ringing Kenny, that Charlie would be fine if given time to calm down, and that he wouldn't hurt me.

Next on her mission was a screwdriver that she had asked me to fetch her from our garage. I asked what she was going to do with it. "I am going to take the locks off your bathroom doors."

"No, please don't do that," I said, thinking of the major hassle that would cause with Joe being a teenager and us all having to use the bathroom. Someone was bound to come when in use before knocking. It fell on deaf ears, and she got the screwdriver and went outside and hid in the front of our house in a bush. I was to give her the nod when Charlie had gone upstairs, which was around twenty minutes later. I opened the door to her, and in she came, and true to her word, took the upstairs and downstairs locks off, adding in a sarcastic tone, "That will put paid to that little trick." With a little grin, she looked at me; that was the one and only time I ever saw something semi-resembled that she was pleased.

Can you believe that I still thought that this must be the right thing to do and that she was showing him a no-nonsense approach? Looking back now, of course, I know that wasn't the right way at all. What an idiot I was! I was so desperate to have help and now I had finally got it. I didn't want to make a fuss. I was all over the place and didn't even know it at the time.

I only saw her once more after that, when I had to go to the hub to pick some paperwork up for Charlie; she said sorry to me, but it was Charlie who was owed an apology. If he wasn't school-phobic before, he certainly was now! She said that I needed to apply for an EHCP (education and health care plan) as when he gets older, he will really hurt you. That was parting words of wisdom. I had tried on several occasions to get the EHCP but had been told, 'You won't get one of them; they are like gold dust, and he wouldn't meet the criteria. Again, I believed that too. I believed everything anyone in authority ever told me back then. God, they must have loved gullible me. I'm pleased to say I'm certainly not so trusting anymore.

CHAPTER SIX

So here we were once more on our own, now that Julie wasn't on the scene anymore. And just to delay things, it was the start of the summer holidays and another year that Charlie had not been in any sort of education.

The first two weeks of the school holidays were dreadful. Charlie was not coming out of his bedroom at all and was so cross and snappy towards me if I tried to even suggest coming downstairs for a little while. I tried to coax him every single day, but the more I pushed him, the more hurtful he would become – swearing at me and pushing me out of his room. One day, in particular, was very testing. I had sat down at the table to start filling in a mountain of paperwork, all Charlie-related, to help him. I had just settled down to make a start and couldn't find my glasses anywhere. I looked in all of the obvious places. Not there! I'm a creature of habit and always left them on the shelf in the living room, so I couldn't understand where on earth they could be.

I went upstairs and asked Joseph if he had seen them. "No, Mum. Where on earth could they be?" I went into Charlie's bedroom and asked him the same question. "Yes, I've seen them."

"Where are they then, Charlie?"

"I've got them," was his reply. "Can I have them back, then, please?"

"No," he stated. So I went over to his chest of drawers to see if they were in there, to which Charlie yelled, "Just get out, piss off, go on, piss off."

"Charlie, I really need them to do this paperwork to help you, please," I almost begged. He just shrugged.

I was feeling so low. What with one thing and another, being shouted and sworn at just cut me to my core. I wasn't strong enough to deal with all of this. Joseph came rushing out of his bedroom and into Charlie's, as he had heard all the commotion, and ordered Charlie to leave me alone and to stop swearing and shouting at me. Joe was really protective of me, more so of late, as he had seen that I wasn't myself at all. This really inflamed the situation, and Charlie went to hit Joseph. All the time, still shouting and swearing, I stood in between them in an attempt to stop the impending fight. But with two big lads, it was impossible. "Please, Joe, leave it," I begged. "You will just make him worse and more angry." But Joseph was having none of it.

So there we all were, me in the middle of the two of them with the palms of my hands on either one's chest, trying and failing to keep them apart. Fists were flying past my head in determination to see who could be the first one to pack a punch. I couldn't hold them for much longer, as my arms were growing weak and heavy, and my resolve was diminishing rapidly. I fell to the floor and curled up into a ball with my hands covering my head, hoping that it would offer some protection for if and when I got caught in the firing line. They both stumbled over me into Charlie's bedroom and crashed onto Charlie's bed with a massive crack. I thought they had broken the bed! The language was just awful, with Charlie screaming all sorts out of his mouth. Spit was flying everywhere in equal measures to match his rage. As quick as it had started, the fight soon burned itself out, thankfully, and Joseph stormed back to his room with a tremendous slam of his door. I know how he felt!

I honestly expected the police to turn up any minute, as the noise had been just horrendous. The poor neighbours must have thought that a murder was being committed. This behaviour continued well into the first two weeks. First, it was my glasses, then the TV remote, magazines, newspapers, reading books, my phone, the house phone, and my house keys were all being hidden on a regular basis. Basically, anything that was mine, he never broke any of my items, just hid them from me. Sometimes, it would take two or three days before he let me have them back. He was developing a very manipulative way about him, almost controlling me and holding my belongings – and me – to ransom until I would give in to his demands that I had previously said no to. Usually, small stuff like sweets, coke, or energy drinks. I didn't mind him having these once or twice a week, but he wanted them every day. Unless I went to the shop for him, that's when the blackmail, banging, and swearing would start until I either gave in and went for him, or he eventually tired himself out and would go to sleep. But I knew it would all start up again once Charlie was awake. I didn't always give in, but on some days when things got particularly bad, I'm afraid to say I did give in to his demands. Those were the days I was at my weakest and could not cope with another day of relentless banging. Sometimes you have to pick your battles. Some might say that I was making a rod for my own back, but until people have been in a similar situation, it's very easy to judge.

Another favourite trick of Charlie's was hiding all the cushions in the house – either behind the sofa and chairs or in the understair cupboard. He certainly seemed to have it in for me, and yet I was the one who was helping him and constantly trying to ring people and organizations for advice. My husband was great when he was at home, but he had to work all hours as he was by now the only earner in the house, which just added to my guilt. Kenny never ever once made me feel that way, though, and he just wished that he could have been around more to help. He hated seeing the state I was in when he got in from work. Very often I could disguise it and put on a smile, and other times I would say, "Oh, I've had a fit of the sneezes," but I don't think he was ever convinced.

Just entering the third week of the holidays, and the banging seemed like it was intensifying. It would be so hard and loud that it would make the pictures on the living room wall vibrate. All the time shouting, "Mum, mum, mum, mum," at the top of his voice. This was by now a regular occurrence of once or twice a day. It would get so bad that I would be sitting downstairs crying and taking my hands through my hair in despair. I would turn the radio on and start vacuuming to try and drown out the constant swearing and shouting. Once things had calmed, I would gingerly go up to see him and check he was okay. Almost immediately, he would start saying, "Well, are you going up the shop then?" and it would start all over again. I just did not know what to do. I was worried about upsetting the neighbours as one side had a young family, and I wondered what they must think with all the swearing. I was worried about my mum, who had very high blood pressure and is also a born worrier. So I would say, "It's okay, Mum, leave it to me." It made me feel worse than ever to think that all this was worrying my lovely, kind mum. I also had to be careful not to worry Kenny too much, as he also had high blood pressure. The situation was taking its toll on all of us.

One afternoon, Kenny had a bad headache, so went for a lie-down. When he came down after a couple of hours, he said that his right eye was blurry but put it down to having not long woken up. He still had a headache, although not as bad. The next morning, being Sunday, his sight still wasn't right in his eye. So first thing Monday, he booked in to see his doctor later that morning. The doctor sent him to the optician, who found a little black dot in the back of Kenny's eye and sent him straight to the eye hospital in Oxford. Further investigations discovered that it was a small blood clot in the back part of his eye. It had cut off the blood supply, and they likened it to a sort of stroke. But instead of the body being affected, this was his vision. The damage, unfortunately, was irreversible, and poor Kenny had lost part of his peripheral vision – both at the bottom part and side part of his eye. He had lots of tests done, and thankfully he passed all of the eye tests. So he was able to keep his driving license, upon which he relied heavily as it was all part of his job as an engineer, and he would travel all over the country. I just couldn't bear the thought of anything happening to Kenny, so I was even more determined not to give him anything to worry about. The doctor said that the clot had been caused by high blood pressure and, yes, you've guessed it... stress!

Still into the third week, and yet again we were having a bad day! I remember that day well as I was just sitting on the sofa staring into space, zombified, when the phone trilled and brought me out of my daze and back to reality. "Hello?"

"Hello, Sharon, it's Richard here, just ringing to see how things are going?" Well, that did it for me. Hearing his calm voice, I just about managed to garble, "Not so good." I went on to tell him of all the awful times Charlie had been through with Julie and how nasty he was being to us all, and in particular myself. I'm not sure how he understood a word I was saying, as I was saying all of it between uncontrollable sobs. I just couldn't help it. It's one thing dealing with this all behind closed doors as you can – or I could – put on a brave face to the outside world. But once you start the process of saying what has been going on, then that is when it all becomes real, and all of the emotions bubble up. The words he said to me next made both sense to me and comforted me. Those wise words were, "Charlie is being hurtful towards you because it's you he trusts, feels safe with, and utterly loves." Although it didn't feel like it at all, it did, however, make perfect sense.

After we had been talking for a while, Richard explained that the very best thing to do for Charlie now was to make sure that he went back to school in September. I agreed wholeheartedly but wondered how on earth this would be achievable. A plan was made that Richard would visit Charlie over the rest of the summer holidays and help get some of his confidence back. It was a great success as Richard visited several times and either played a board game with him or, if Charlie felt able, had a kickabout with his football over the park. I could not thank Richard enough. After all, it was his time off also, but he said he didn't mind at all, and the most important thing was to put the past behind us and look forward to a new start in September. Richard had such a calm way about him that he very soon won Charlie's confidence, and once again, I slowly began to see a tiny glimmer of the old Charlie emerging with the beautiful smile and kindness he showed his beloved pets. Still, he wasn't coming out of his bedroom, but as long as he was in a better place mentally, then working on coming out of his room could be dealt with another time.

The first day of school arrived in September, and Kenny once again had taken a few days off to help with the settling-in period. That first morning went great as we helped Charlie get organized. And just as he said, Richard was waiting for Charlie outside what would be his classroom and year six, the final year at primary school. We all introduced ourselves, and his new teacher introduced us to a teaching assistant called Mrs. Card, who was to be Charlie's support during the school day. Both teachers were very kind and had lovely, genuine smiles. Kenny and I said our goodbyes and left, and I felt as though this could be it. At long last, we had cracked it between us all. I went back at lunchtime to collect Charlie, as had been arranged for that first week. "Was it good, Charlie?" I dared hardly ask. "Yes, Mum, it was." I would've given him the biggest squeeze and kiss ever, but that is one of the things Charlie had always hated, so I didn't want to push my luck.

The next morning, he went off fine with me on the bus, and then again the next morning and the next. We were on a roll. I almost skipped with joy on the walk home from school. I now totally understood the saying "walking on air!" All was well. We still had the odd blip along the way sometimes, like one morning, he really didn't want to go to school, and when we got off the bus, he thought that it would be a great idea to run away from me. Just as he started to stomp off and a cold panic had begun to descend on me, the wonderful Mrs Card just happened to be turning into the school in her car. So, thank God she was able to talk him round with her usual kind, humorous, but no-nonsense way. As soon as she said, "Charlie Norman, what's going on?" his face would lighten, and he would start to go red in the face, with a little smile appearing at the same time. She reassured him all would be okay, and off he went with her to school like a little lamb. What a huge difference having the right help and support made.

The other time that Charlie decided to scare the life very nearly out of me was when he was doing his cycle provisional training. For a few weeks, we would have to bike the two miles to school, as I didn't have any other means of transporting his bike there. Now, I hadn't ridden a bike for about twenty years, so to say I was a tad rusty was being very generous indeed. Halfway to school, so about one mile into the journey, we have to cross two extremely busy main roads that have a small island in the middle for a crossing point. Charlie was a good rider and was way ahead of me. I, on the other hand, could barely keep in a straight line, and my bike was very big and heavy and very old-fashioned, so it was really hard work. I was trying but failing to keep up with Charlie. I was pedalling fast but getting very far at all, all the while trying to keep on my bike and navigate where on earth Charlie was. I tried shouting his name, but between me being out of puff and the constant roar of the traffic, this proved fruitless. Once I made it to the two busy roads, there was still no sign of Charlie. I took it he must have got across the roads unscathed as the traffic was all still flowing. "Thank God!" I said out loud. Just over from the busy roads is a cycle track down a lane with no cars at all, and the track takes you the remainder of the mile and more or less comes out right outside the school grounds. I stopped briefly to scan the path and still couldn't see him. My heart by now was going so fast as I had no clue where he was, but I did know that he wouldn't have carried on to school without me. Your mind speeds up in situations like this, and I must have imagined every scenario in every police drama that I had ever watched! Charlie is vulnerable, and if a stranger had asked him to go with him or her, then he more than likely would have, as he just wouldn't have been able to speak and say no.

Then I caught sight of him through the hedge on a housing estate, cycling back in the opposite direction and, more worryingly, back toward the busy main road and home. I dumped my bike as it was quicker for me to run after him. I was yelling, "Stop, Charlie, please stop!" Did he stop? Did he? Heck, he still kept on going and was getting nearer and nearer the busy rush hour road. I could barely look and just prayed that he would stop. Just as I got to the road, his dad happened to be going past in his work van on his way to another job. If ever there was a time when I needed my guardian angel, she came good that day, just when I needed her. Before Charlie knew it, his dad had stopped him in his tracks, took the bike, put it in the back of his van and put Charlie in the front seat. Kenny said that he would see me at the schools; I still had my bike to go back for.

So, apart from those couple of incidents and the odd times Charlie got persuaded to do some silly childish pranks by the other lads in his class, all in good humour, I must add, all went well. He had made a few friends and even went back to their houses for tea on a few occasions and vice versa. Charlie would invite them to ours. It was lovely to see Charlie being like any other boy his age. Even when I did get called in about the childish behaviour, I couldn't tell him off too much. He had a lot of catching up to do after all, and it was never anything serious. His teacher was great and always told me and nipped it in the bud after she had spoken to him, and all was forgotten. It was a really lovely school; it had a family feel to it and a comforting atmosphere.

At around Christmas time, just as Charlie had turned eleven, I thought that I had better start making some arrangements for Charlie's transition up to the secondary school, which was just next door. I hadn't given up on the idea of an EHCP, so I made an appointment with the primary school's SENCO (special educational needs coordinator). She was a very approachable lady, so I felt comfortable and at ease talking with her, and by now, I had faith that they all wanted the best for Charlie as well. I went into the meeting all upbeat and confident about the EHCP application process but came deflated and downbeat as the SENCO explained that there was no way Charlie would meet the criteria for an EHCP assessment, as he was doing so well at school and that there wouldn't be any need for one. I explained that I was looking and thinking ahead, and as Charlie was scheduled to go to the mainstream secondary school in September, I was very worried that without this important legally binding document, things would soon come crashing down again.

I felt this document would help Charlie immensely and would last until he was twenty-five years old, so it would give Charlie the opportunity to be able to access the help he so badly needed. In my opinion, this wasn't just about his academic side but also his health and well-being, so obtaining an EHCP would tie all of this together. This had been a very difficult few years and had impacted hugely on Charlie's mental health, and I really felt that this would be of benefit. But after explaining all of this to the SENCO, the same answer prevailed, which was still a firm "Sorry, but no!" Back then, I had no idea that I could have, as the parent, applied for an EHCP myself on behalf of Charlie, and nobody ever told me, or else I would have applied myself. It's a good thing, I always think, if the school can apply as it adds more clout in my opinion. Although you can always appeal the decision if the LA (local authority) denies your child an assessment, as most appeals are successful, they are definitely worth the stress of going through. Wrong as that is and shouldn't happen; unfortunately, it does happen. Being a parent of a disabled or special needs child is worrying enough without the stress that the local authority can sometimes put you through. My advice now to anyone going through this is never, ever give up. If you are told no, pursue it yourself, either on your own or with the support of SENDIAS or your local care centre. I wish I had known this, but as it was, I went away from the meeting disappointed but accepting of the decision.

Charlie got his place at the mainstream secondary school, and well before his start date, he had a few visits with his teaching assistant. Richard had also arranged with both schools that Mrs. Card could go up to the secondary school with Charlie for the first three months. So, from September to December, he would have great support during this important settling-in period. As you can imagine, we were all over the moon at this news and knew just how much it would help Charlie as he absolutely adored Mrs. Card. We were so grateful and appreciated all that Richard and the school had done for Charlie and us as a family. So come July, Charlie said a sad goodbye to his class teacher and also to some of his friends who would be going on to different schools. We were all happy and in a good headspace. What could possibly go wrong?

CHAPTER SEVEN

So here we were in early September 2013, and eleven-year-old Charlie's first day at secondary school. He looked so smart, all decked out in his new uniform—black trousers, white shirt, black jumper, tie, and blazer. We couldn't have been prouder of him. We were both smiling at how grown-up he looked. The only one not smiling was Charlie himself. When it was time to leave, he looked scared and vulnerable. Kenny took the obligatory first-day-at-school photo, and to say that the camera never lies was never truer on this day. I still have it on my phone, and it captures just how anxious he must have felt.

With much reassurance that Mrs. Card would meet us at the school and stay with him, it really gave him the push he needed. He found the uniform very scratchy and uncomfortable, but not wanting to appear different from the other new children, he just about managed to tolerate it, albeit with him scratching at his legs and wiggling his neck and shoulders around, trying to free himself from the feeling of being strangled by the starchy collar and tie.

So, lunch packed into a new lunch bag, rucksack on his back, pencil case, exercise book, and the basic mobile phone we had bought for him, we were all ready to go. Again, Kenny had taken a few days off from work to ease the worry of the bus and to help support myself and, of course, Charlie. It was also a great comfort for us all that Joseph attended the same school. He would be going into year nine, so they could get the school bus together. Joe would also be on hand if Charlie, for whatever reason, needed him. They were, by now, thankfully getting on much better. Still, the odd bust-up, as all young brothers do, but on the whole, Joseph had a much better understanding of autism and was more tolerant of his brother.

I made sure once or twice a month that I would spend time with Joe, just the two of us, either going into Oxford on the bus and treating him to lunch out or a new top or jeans or even just walking together over the fields where we lived. Then, at night, we would have an easy TV dinner and watch a film. I would like to say all of us, but sadly, Charlie preferred staying in his room playing his computer games.

Now that the atmosphere was somewhat lighter, I felt quietly confident that things would go smoothly on the first days of school. And I am very pleased to say that they did. His teaching assistant was always there to meet Charlie before the bell rang at the start of the school day. For two blissful weeks, all was good. Charlie was going to school for the first time in a very, very long while and all without too much stress for him, which in turn was far less stress for all of our household. He still came home with a splitting headache and looking very pale, but after having a cuddle with his two rabbits Bertie and Bessie and playing with our Border Collie dog Bonnie, he would be calmer and would flop out onto his bed and fall asleep. He was totally exhausted.

Despite all of this, he was still going. Then I got a phone call that made my stomach flip. The sort of flip you get when going over a humpback bridge, and my blood turned ice-cold like a wave going over me. The reason being is that I could not believe what was going to happen! I can't even remember who called me, but I would imagine one of the schools. Those dreadful words echoed around my head, "I am afraid, Mrs. Jeacock, but we will be asking Mrs. Card to leave Charlie and come back to her position in the primary school as she is needed."

"No, no, please, no. She was to be with Charlie for three months," I gushed. "Sorry, nothing we can do," very closely followed by "It is reported that Charlie is doing so well... flying, in fact! So it is felt that she has been successful in her job already to transition Charlie."

Well, I was struck dumb, and I just could not comprehend what this person was telling me. I eventually found my voice and said, "Can't you see the reason he is flying is because of the help and support he is getting, and now it's being taken away?" Again, I was met with "Sorry, that's just how it is." I rang the school immediately to make sure that they had a suitable teaching assistant to take over supporting Charlie. "Oh yes, there is always a teaching assistant floating in class should he need one." But Charlie used to have a one-to-one. The reply beggars belief: "Well, he won't get a one-to-one without an EHCP... Argh! What an absolute joke," I thought inwardly.

Both Kenny and I could hardly believe the irony of it all. I then had the dreadful task of breaking this news to Charlie. Talk about a roller coaster for the poor lad. As expected, he was beside himself that his helper and greatest supporter that he had ever had was to be leaving him. I tried my best to keep things positive and upbeat for him and explained that everyone was pleased with how he was doing and how well he was coping. He nodded in agreement. That can't always be relied upon as, where Charlie is concerned, he will very often answer with what he thinks you want to hear, so in turn, in his mind, it is the end of the conversation.

As expected, the next morning, Charlie was extra quiet and very short-tempered with me, something that had seldom happened of late. Joe, Charlie, and I all set off for the bus stop, and once we were on board, Charlie began to look really unwell. He was sitting all on his own at the front of the bus. He always preferred to be sat alone, but I was aware of all the other children having fun, laughing and joking amongst themselves as they did every morning. But this morning, it seemed to stand out even more just how out of things Charlie was—a stark reminder, seeing his scared, frightened, pale little face. God, I wish he was sat at the back of the bus, joining in with the fun. I can feel the tears pricking at my eyes even now at the very memory of it. It must have been horrendous for him, even more so that morning, as he wouldn't have his beloved Mrs. Card.

We arrived at school, and I watched as Charlie walked into school with his brother. Then, I began the two-mile walk back home. I hadn't been in the door for five minutes when the phone rang. "Hello, Mrs. Jeacock?" My heart sank as the lady went on to say, "Can you come and pick Charlie, please? He has been sick."

"What a surprise," I thought sarcastically but instead replied with, "Yes, of course. Give me half an hour, and I will be there." So, I began the two-mile walk back to the school. I would get us both a taxi home, but I couldn't afford both ways, plus they would charge waiting time.

When I entered the reception, there sat a very tired and pale-looking Charlie. "Oh, Charlie, bless your heart," I went to give him a big hug, but Charlie gave his usual "Get off me" shrug. Still, one of the hardest parts for me to accept is that Charlie doesn't like hugs or kisses. As a mother's instinct, that's all you want to do when your child is upset, hurt, or for a happy celebrational hug.

The taxi arrived, and we soon arrived back home. Once he had a sleep, I asked him what did he thought had made him sick? Of course, I knew fine well what it was, and it had all bubbled up and overwhelmed him. Charlie really struggles to articulate his feelings, but he did manage to tell me that he had a really bad headache and tummy ache, felt lost and confused, and then was sick. I had still packed in his rucksack his help cards with pictures of feelings on them, but when Charlie reaches that level of anxiety, all of what we have told him about the cards goes from his mind. I can't even begin what that level of fear must feel like for an eleven-year-old boy, who just desperately wants to be the same as his peers. Heartbreaking. "Well done for managing to tell me, Charlie," I said gently.

The next morning was the same, and the next and the next! In fact, most mornings after that, I would get a call to say that Charlie had been sick and could I go to reception to pick him up. After around two weeks, I mentioned that maybe Charlie could go to a quiet area or go to see the pastoral care lady, as I knew it was anxiety. Where I certainly didn't mind going to fetch him, I felt that a pattern was forming, which wasn't doing Charlie any good whatsoever. Just an idea that I thought Charlie would have responded well to, but they didn't think that idea would work or even be possible. Plus, school rules state that if you are sick, then you have to go home. "But this isn't some sort of bug; it's anxiety sickness," I stated. Although they were sympathetic, nothing constructive was being suggested in terms of moving forward.

On week three of Charlie feeling sick or actually being sick, I had walked back home after the school drop-off and turned my ankle over badly. Although I could walk short distances, no way would I be able to walk the two miles to pick him up today. So when the inevitable phone call came, I explained my predicament and gave them my permission to ring a taxi for Charlie to bring him home to me, and I would pay once they got here. After some time, maybe half an hour, I received a text from Charlie with the following: "I don't know where I am, Mum." My stomach did its usual flip as I texted back, "Why? What do you mean?" Then decided I would ring him to see what had happened. No answer! So, I texted back as quickly as I could, "Why are you not answering your phone, Charlie?" Thank goodness he replied straight back, "Because I don't want to talk in front of the taxi man." Poor Charlie. "Can you recognize whereabouts you are, Charlie?" Charlie texts back, "Well, we went past our house, and now we are going out of the village to the other end." I rang the main office of the taxi firm after getting the number from the school. I explained as best I could in my rushed, semi-panicked way, "Don't worry," they reassured me and rang through to the driver and gave him more direct instructions to exactly which house we lived in. Seemingly the driver had asked Charlie, "Which house is yours?" and just as Charlie had told me, he couldn't speak. Charlie honestly thought that he was being abducted. Hence that was the first and last time that he has ever been in a taxi on his own again.

After the taxi incident, it was just impossible for me to get Charlie into school. He did do the odd morning here and there, but I was always called in to come and fetch him. I spoke to CAMHS, who were going to arrange some CBT therapy for Charlie, but he had tried that countless times before, and it hadn't been a great success for him. In my eyes, it was so simply solved—he needed a teaching assistant to support him as that is the only thing that had ever worked in the past. Why on earth no one else could see it was beyond me. Whenever I had mentioned it as a solution, it was always met with great amusement of "Ha, wouldn't all of our students love their very own TA?" I could clearly see I was losing the battle, but I was determined. All that Charlie had been through, and I most definitely would not be losing the fight for him... ever!

I tried in our defence that I'm sure that every student would like their own TA, but this wasn't about like this was about need! So, after doing two whole weeks of year seven, that was more or less it, as I did not count the dribs and drabs of the following two weeks. And yet another year without any education. Year eight by now was fast approaching too fast, and yes, you've guessed it— Charlie didn't even attempt to go, as things had gone way past that point, and now he couldn't go as much as he wanted to. This time, I can't say I blamed him.

I rang the school, and the only thing that suddenly concerned them was his attendance marks, which came as no surprise to me, were seriously low. I imagine there must be an Ofsted inspection looking for the sudden interest, I thought cynically. It wouldn't have made any difference to Charlie if the Queen herself was visiting school—wild horses couldn't have got him there. Believe me, despite everything, I still persevered every single morning to get him to go to school. I was worried I would get a fine, or have to have a court appearance or worse, even prison. It's emotionally draining caring for someone with mental health issues along with autism and all of Charlie's other health needs, and it was all starting to take its toll on me once again. Silly things at first, like going upstairs but forgetting what for; everybody does that from time to time, so I didn't really pay much attention to it. I think most of the time, I was in such a daze of worry and ringing people that I couldn't concentrate properly. I was still ringing school every morning, but it was like they had just forgotten about Charlie, as if he had dropped off the face of the earth. No wonder he felt so low, my lovely boy; I hated seeing him so flat and deflated.

I rang SENDIAS again, who have always been a great support, and they said that they would arrange a meeting ASAP as this had gone on long enough. I also rang the Missing in Education team to let them know that Charlie had been out of education for a very long time. She seemed to take it all in and made all the right encouraging noises, but again, nothing came of it. A meeting eventually took place, and it was a total utter waste of time, as the only pearls of wisdom that they could offer were, "We know Charlie finds school trousers uncomfortable; buy him some lycra cycling long pants to put underneath."

"Hey presto!" The cure-all. Why hadn't I thought of that? I thought to myself inwardly. I honestly did not know what to do or where to turn, whether to laugh or cry at the frustration of it all. It was just ludicrous. SENDIAS were a great help verbally to me in the meeting, and they came up with some good strategies, but the bottom line was that Charlie needed to be in school for those strategies to be implemented.

Another two months passed with no school when I had an arranged visit from the attendance office along with the lady from pastoral care. The attendance officer was a tall, portly man, nice enough, but he turned everything into a joke, maybe to ease my nerves, but I was long past joking. I thought they might offer a solution, and now that they were in my home, they could see for themselves just how affected Charlie was. They did offer me a solution, and guess what it was? A parenting course! I had already done two of those in the early days of Charlie's diagnosis. I turned it down with a "thanks, but no thanks." It's very easy to pass the blame onto the parents, and then they can walk away, conscious-free of this awful, dreadful situation. I already felt like a performing seal; I had jumped through so many hoops, and I was not going to be jumping anymore. CAMHS thankfully spoke to the school and backed up my claim that it was not my parenting skills that were at fault.

All this was driving me crazy; I was so drained myself, and my forgetfulness was still bothering me. I was very tired with worry to the point of feeling sick, and yet nobody knew the true extent of our situation. I could go from crying my eyes out to a beaming smile within seconds, and nobody was any the wiser. It's my own fault, I know, but I felt so tired I really didn't want to go into it all. I had some lovely friends who would've only been too pleased to listen; some people were opinionated and, of course, knew best and would often look at me like I had grown two heads and say, "What do you mean, you can't get him to go to school?" Another really helpful one is "Autism? He doesn't look it." Another well-meaning one, "Don't worry, Shaz, he will be fine."

One Saturday, Kenny suggested that I take Bonnie, our dog, for a walk to clear my head. He knew how much I liked walking; it would usually help me analyse things better. But on this walk, it didn't quite go the way I was hoping. I had walked a long way across many fields, again crying to myself at what was going to happen. It was the only way I could get my emotions out in private without worrying anyone at home. The floodgates opened, and I let it all out and even had a scream in frustration. When I had stopped crying, the most peculiar thing happened. I did not have a clue where I was. I looked around and didn't recognize a single thing. Now, I had walked these fields my entire life and knew it like the back of my hand.

What was going on? I was starting to really panic. I sat down on the grass and stroked my dog as she was licking my face. I took some deep breaths and talked myself into a calm state of reasoning. Slowly standing up, I began to get my bearings, and as quick as they had gone, they came thankfully back, and I was able to navigate my way home. It really scared me; I thought I had gone mad. I've since learned after it happened again, which I will get to later in this book, that it is all to do with how your brain processes stress, a bit like a safety mechanism.

Since Charlie had been off school, his temperament had been better, especially with me. I now know that it is because I had stopped fighting him in the mornings to get ready. It wasn't that I had lost the will to fight; this time I was fighting for him and not against him, trying to force him to go. It achieved nothing but unnecessary upset. He was scared, not obstinate or naughty, and in my opinion, that should not be punished, only nurtured and constructive on how we were going to move forward. In order to achieve that, I needed school to at least try and help him.

I called for another meeting with the school, and present were Kenny, the class teacher, pastoral care, Richard, and myself. The school attendance officer was invited but declined; he was busy. After much talking and me doing the usual crying, it was decided that Charlie would have a place in the school's inclusion unit, which was a bungalow within the school grounds and was a purpose-used building to help students like Charlie who needed that bit of extra help and support. Why this hadn't been suggested to us before now, I shall never know, but it had, and we were all extremely pleased. To start with, it would be for one hour per day for three mornings a week, which was welcomed news as Charlie's energy levels were very low from being so inactive for so long. He would have a teaching assistant who would come to our home to visit Charlie a few times to get to know him and then slowly introduce him to the bungalow. Alongside this, Richard had arranged for one of his team, an autism mentor, to visit Charlie at home to do some therapy with him.

We met the T.A., Carol, and she was so nice and very kind. She used to be a nurse, so she had a good understanding of Charlie's health needs. Carol would pick us both up in her car and take us to school. Then, I would leave them both for an hour before returning back for Charlie. It wasn't worth me going home as by the time it would have taken me to walk home; it would be time to start heading back. There was a Co-op shop just on the opposite side of the school, so I would wander around and buy a newspaper. I must have looked a bit dodgy just browsing for ages. If the weather was good, I would go to the local park and read the paper. That soon passed away the hour, but with the typical English weather, that didn't happen too many times. I didn't mind one bit, though, as this was all helping Charlie, and I would have stood in the rain all day long to achieve that for him.

On Fridays, we were to meet the autism mentor for the first time. I must admit I was a tad apprehensive after the Julie experience, but I need not have worried. Floortje, or Flo as she liked to be called, was absolutely wonderful. She had such a calm, relaxing way about her, and both Charlie and I warmed to her straight away. She was so very gentle with Charlie and would very often start her session with some relaxation exercises. It was so relaxing that Charlie's eyes would close, and I myself could easily have fallen asleep too. It was amazing! After a while, things progressed to the three of us having a few games of frustration (aptly named!). Charlie loved this game and won almost every game, which added to his glee.

Things were continuing to go well at school, so his hour was increased to two hours three times a week, which meant I just about had enough time to walk to the local town, do a bit of shopping, and walk back in plenty of time to meet Charlie. Then, after a good few months, Flo told us the sad news that she would be leaving but had arranged for another member of the mentor team to take her place. She wouldn't be leaving for another few weeks but wanted to let Charlie know in good time so he could process the news. We were, of course, very sad, but once Flo had left, we kept in touch and are still friends to this day. The next time Flo visited, she brought her replacement with her, Lorna, and just like Flo, we both warmed to her instantly. Whereas Flo was very gentle and calm, Lorna was very bubbly and chatty, so they complemented each other perfectly. Charlie particularly loved her sense of humour, and it was impossible to be sad and down with Lorna around.

Just before Flo's last visit with Lorna, we had a meeting arranged with the school that was to be at my house. Present were Flo, Lorna, Charlie, myself, the TA, and the school SENCO, whom I hadn't met before. They arrived, and we did the usual introductions. What the SENCO said next certainly didn't make me warm to her! The words were, "Right, Charlie, you will soon be in year nine, so it's time for you to go back into the main school, full time." The look on all of our faces must have spoken volumes. As quick as a flash, I said, "No." Followed by "Why?"

"Because Charlie is getting a big boy now," she said rather condescendingly I felt. The rest of the meeting is a bit of a blur. All I really remember is a strong feeling of déjà vu.

I asked a few days later how the EHCP application was coming along, as it had been a good two or three months since the application had been suggested in the meeting. I knew that these things take time, but I wanted to give them a nudge as we hadn't heard. The reply was, "Oh yes, we've been advised not to pursue it as there is not enough evidence." I could not speak, struck dumb with amazement, and at no point did anyone tell me that I could apply. I was beyond mad. Later, I spoke with Lorna and Richard, and in turn, they made some phone calls to put things back in motion. But this huge hiccup had put the whole process back by months, and as predicted, Charlie was unable to attend school at the start of year nine. How could he? When he had been so well supported within the inclusion centre, and now that he was a 'big boy in year nine, he was expected to go back into full-time mainstream. Absolutely no way would or should he cope with that.

Thank goodness we still had Lorna, who could lighten the days that she visited. Even on our darkest days, she would never fail to raise a smile or two. One day that will forever stick in my mind was one morning when Charlie had started his shouting and banging directed at me. As I was still so run down and low, it didn't take long before I dissolved in tears. I put the hoover on and started the vacuuming and turned the radio up as I had done many times before. I was still aware of the banging in the background when the doorbell rang. My first thought was "Oh god, who is it?" With my eyes like two swollen slits, I did not want to be confronted by anyone at all. I had to answer it as it was more than apparent that someone was in with all of the commotion going on. It was Lorna! And she took one look at me and said, "Oh Sharon, come here," and then gave me the biggest, warmest hug ever. Charlie had gone suddenly quiet as he knew it was Lorna. She went up and had one of her chats with him and worked her magic. I will never forget that impromptu visit. It came just at the right time and will stay in my memory always.

CHAPTER EIGHT

With all of these years that had passed, we were now in January 2017, and Charlie had just turned fifteen in December. Charlie's teaching assistant and the new SENCO, who was much more understanding, came around to our house to, at long last, start the application for the EHCP. Thankfully, the application went through all the stages, and it was approved without a quibble, which saved us the drawn-out task of an appeal process. I was so desperately keen to obtain this document as it would enable Charlie to access the help that he so needed and would give him a chance to attend a more suitable school that could meet his needs. I had already started to have a look around with Charlie, and we visited some very good settings. The one that Charlie preferred was a mainstream school which had an autism resources base within the grounds of the school. The winning factor for Charlie was that this school had a farm and a forest school so it would be just perfect for him. Now that we had the 'gold dust' EHCP all done and dusted, we got the go-ahead that he could start at this new school, and they said that they could meet Charlie's needs. It all sounded perfect. This school was around fifteen miles away, as were all the other resource centres that we had looked at. So, I had to apply to the county council for transport, which again was granted.

This was going to be a huge undertaking for Charlie, so I was very relieved to hear that Lorna would take Charlie for the first few weeks to get him used to going to school first. Then, she would do some work with him in order to try and lessen his anxiety around going in the taxi. Charlie would be put on a part-time timetable, which would be three mornings per week. In the meantime, the chap who ran the taxi firm and would also be Charlie's driver very kindly came to visit us at home along with his wife, who was the taxi's escort and travelled in the back to watch over the students. It was so nice of him to come and see Charlie as he wanted to put Charlie's mind at ease and say hi to him. He even brought his drone over and took lots of airborne pictures of our house and garden. He certainly went above and beyond to help reassure Charlie.

Lorna had made some picture cards that indicated "I feel sick" or "I'm worried," and such like, as Charlie was still unable to articulate in words his feelings. When he went with Lorna, he would be okay and went in with no problem. But sadly, her time with him was soon due to end as she had already spent more time with Charlie than her job role stated she should. So the sooner Charlie went willingly in the taxi, the better it would be all around. It was a shared taxi with four or five other students who were picked up from all over the local area. A couple of the other students were very vocal and sweaty, understandably, as they all had special needs at various levels, so it couldn't be helped at all. But this really unsettled Charlie and scared him as he was such a quiet lad. So inevitably, Charlie was sick, and he wasn't able to use his picture cards. That's how crippling his anxiety could be, poor, poor boy. It must have been agony for him. He was sick several more times, both in the taxi and at school, which resulted in... Yes, you've guessed it, school refusal. Incidentally, I hate that terminology of school refusal, as it makes it sound as though the child/young person is being defiant in refusing to go when, mostly, in my experience, it's a real phobia. All Charlie ever wanted was to go to school.

We were referred by CAMHS to the crisis outreach team, which is another form of CAMHS, but you have to reach a crisis point to be able to access them, which is ludicrous, but there you are. Lorna stayed with us for a few more sessions to meet the new person who would be helping Charlie from the crisis team. As it happened, it was the most lovely young lady called Clair. She was very young, maybe in her early twenties, but she really knew her stuff, and both Charlie and myself warmed to her. We were all on the same page and wanted what was best for my son. It was a really sad day when Lorna had to leave. She had gotten me through some very hard days, and we would miss her so much, but we stayed in touch and are still firm friends to this day. Clair would be with us for around a year, which was music to my ears. Clair would be doing lots of work with Charlie around his anxiety. At first, she would get Charlie as far as the front door, and this would be repeated every visit until Charlie wasn't so anxious and didn't feel sick or shaky. Once he had mastered that, Clair would then walk down our path with him, then sit in her car, going a bit further each time until they finally made the half-hour journey to the school. They were doing fantastically well together, and both worked so hard.

Alongside this therapy, the school had arranged for his teacher and head of the base to come out every morning at seven a.m. to help Charlie calm down and get him in a more positive mindset for trying to go to school. Linda would drive him to the base and bring him home again at lunchtime. This started in September 2017, and Linda would be coming for three mornings per week. All was going really well with both Chloe working in conjunction with the teacher. I really felt like we were getting somewhere, which we were, until just after Christmas 2018. So, three months after Linda's first visit, I received a telephone call to say she wouldn't be able to come anymore.

"What, not at all?" I inquired. "No, that was it, no more visits," came the reply. "Why?" I wanted to know what had changed. "We are extremely short-staffed, and I cannot be spared anymore," she said. "Oh no! Will someone else be taking over from you?" I asked, thinking about all that hard work which had been done so far and the thought of us getting to know another new face was daunting. Charlie was going to feel so let down over this latest obstacle. Linda promised me that someone else would be appointed to work with Charlie but warned me it may take a while to set things in motion. I knew it couldn't be helped, but God, I was mad. I thanked Linda for all of her help so far and that I would look forward to hearing from her to find out who and when the other replacement would start. Her parting words were, "Don't forget to ring or text into school to let them know if Charlie isn't going to come in."

"Well, of course, he isn't going to go in; he isn't going to jump in his taxi and appear suddenly!" But I politely replied, "No, I won't."

While Clair had managed to get Charlie as far as the school gates, she wasn't actually allowed to take him into the grounds of the school, which seemed crazy to us both. I can't quite remember the ins and outs of why, but I guess it had something to do with policies or something along those lines. Clair still drove him there every visit and was really building up Charlie's confidence. Having heard nothing from the school for

Over two weeks, despite me ringing in every morning like I was instructed to do, I rang and asked what was happening. "I'm sorry, it is manic here. It's taking longer to sort something out," was the response. Not wanting to appear pushy, I thought I would give them another two weeks, as I know what it's like to be short-staffed and thought the last thing they would want is me on the phone. So, another two weeks passed and still nothing. So, yet again, I rang and was told more or less the same thing, except this time they said a TA had lined up to take over, but she might have a transport issue as she didn't have a car! I would say that that was a huge problem!

Thinking that I had been more than generous with still no joy, I rang SENDIAS, and I also rang Charlie's SEN Officer at the county council. I followed this up with an email. Thank goodness I did, which will become apparent later on. I explained via email that the EHCP isn't being followed. SENDIAS also left emails and made an attempt to telephone her and leave messages. We still didn't hear back from her. I must have sent at least ten emails by now. As I've stated before, I don't like, in fact, hate making a fuss, but this was just dreadful, unprofessional practice. By now, it was June 2018, so six months since the school couldn't help my son. I had not heard anything despite all the calls and emails. In the end, SENDIAS asked or demanded an emergency annual review of the EHCP. While we were waiting for the meeting to be arranged, both Kenny and I had 'the talk' with Charlie to make sure that he still would like to go to school, and the answer was always the same: "Yes, I really do."

I knew that he liked this new school as he always went with Lorna. He particularly loved the goats as they would run up to greet him and give him a gentle bunt. He would stand for ages stroking their heads and was just so fascinated with the feel of the goats' horns. One goat, in particular, was very keen on chewing Charlie's sleeve, which Charlie found highly amusing. It was so lovely to see him happy and relaxed with the animals. Apart from the goats, they had chickens, ducks, horses, cows, sheep, and lambs. Lorna took lots of photos of Charlie with the goats so that if he was feeling anxious about going, he could look at those pictures to help make him feel calmer. So, we were all desperate, including Charlie, to have this meeting and move forward.

It was during this waiting game that I was encouraged to join the social media page Facebook. I was a bit apprehensive at first, but I am so pleased that Kenny talked me into it as not only did it help me reconnect with friends, but it also enabled me to join lots of different support groups about mental health in children. Another one was autism support, a page called School Refusal Help and Advice, and Parenting Mental Health were a wealth of knowledge and help. I was taken aback at just how many parents out there were having the same time as our family. I had previously thought that countrywide, there must be hundreds in a similar boat, but now I've looked, I'm talking thousands, and that's just one group! Part of me found this a comfort, but the other half made me very sad and angry that this was going on and, worse still, being hidden. Nobody seemed to care about all of these families and all the children out there who were 'out of sight, out of mind' like our Charlie had been for so many years.

It was in one of these groups that a poor woman asked for advice as she had run out of options and was, by this time, at the end of her tether. Her child had been out of school for about four months, and rightly so she was up in arms about it and asked what could she do? Of course, this thread caught my attention immediately as it was very close to what we were going through. So, I waited with bated breath for the answers to come flooding in. What I read and learned made me feel both empowered and very annoyed, as under Section 19 of the Education Act reads as follows:

"The right to a suitable education: what the law says. Section 19. Education Act (1996) "Each local authority shall make arrangements for the provision of suitable education at school or otherwise than at school for those children of compulsory school age who, by reason of illness, exclusion from school or otherwise, may not for any period receive suitable education unless such arrangements are made for them" The statement is clear: the LA must provide suitable education for a child who is out-of-school ill, excluded, 'or otherwise.' This duty applies to all children, whether they have special educational needs (SEN) or not. The education provided must also be full-time unless the LA determines that it would not be in the child's best interest to do so due to their physical or mental health. Section 19 also signposts the LA to seek further direction from any statutory guidance published by the secretary of state. Section 42 Children with Educational, Health and Care Plans (EHCP) have further protection under the Children and Families Act (2014) "The local authority must secure special educational provision for the child or young person." It goes on and on, but the general gist is that my son could have had a home tutor for the past five years. They had let him down massively, and I was darn sure they weren't going to get away with it.

We got a date for the meeting, and with my new knowledge and fire in my belly, I felt the most confident that I had ever felt going into a meeting before. Present at the meeting were Kenny, myself, Clair, Lorna, who had come to offer the input that she had put in, a lady from SENDIAS, Emily, whom Clair had invited from the locality hub; she was part of the MASH team (multi-agency safeguarding hub), Linda the leader of the base, the deputy headmaster, and the SEN officer from the local authority. They were all smiles and sickly sweet to me, my husband, and each other, which I found incredibly cringe-worthy and false, making small talk while we waited for the meeting to start. Thank goodness that I had Lorna and Chloe here for support if need be.

In all other meetings, I have always cried, sometimes even before all the introductions had been made. They knew this, so they would always start with me, the weakest link, so then they could try and manipulate what I wanted to say. Still, they couldn't always get it out of my mouth either through nerves, crying, or, more than likely, both! So once the formal stuff was out of the way, the headmaster said, "Right then, shall we get started?" He sat very casually, crossed-legged, and his right hand draped over the chair next to him. He was sitting very laid back, almost slumped in his hardback school chair. "Mum, shall we start with you? How do you think things are going?" I looked across at the deputy head, who by this time was almost horizontal in his chair. For a second, I was sure that I saw smugness etched across his face, which really riled me up.

"Mum thinks it's going dreadfully and that our son has been failed appallingly for years! And I want to know what you are all going to do about all of the failings?" I scanned the room as if directing it to all; the head suddenly sat up straight in his chair and looked at the base leader for an answer, who, in turn, looked at the SEN Officer. Basically, everyone was looking at each other, shuffling paperwork, and frantically tapping away on a laptop. I could feel my face throbbing with emotion and rage; I could literally feel it pulsing. My heart felt like it was going to come out of my chest; I swear I could feel it touching my ribs. While I was still on a roll, I added, "Why hasn't my son had the education that he is legally entitled to? And why has no replacement been found for the home visits?" I was feeling so angry but tried my best to keep composed.

The deputy said, "We are short-staffed, as has been explained to you already, Mrs. Jeacock."

"I appreciate that totally, but if that is the case, did you inform the local authority? And if so, why hasn't anything been put in place? And if you haven't informed the LA, why not?" Either way, both the school and LA had failed our son. What the deputy head said then blew my mind: "We knew that we couldn't meet his needs a year ago!" This just about pushed all of my buttons at once. "So why the heck weren't you honest about it at the time? Instead, you chose not to be honest and have wasted not only Charlie's time but that of Lorna and Chloe. Chloe could have spent the past year getting him ready for a school that could meet his needs." Of course, he totally bypassed answering that, instead saying, "We want you to sign so we can off-role Charlie from our school."

"No way am I doing that." Luckily, SENDIAS had given me the heads up as they guessed they would want to go down that route. If I had signed to off-role, then I would basically be signing away any help that this school should be offering. Although this was zero, they still had a legal obligation to help find a school that could meet his needs. Also, I suspect the real reason for the off-rolling was that there was an Ofsted inspection looming, and they would or should have noticed the huge gaps in Charlie's absences. It would not look good on the school or on him. "I will be getting in touch with our MP over the failings, and I will be seeking legal advice," I informed the room, and as quick as a flash, the deputy retorted, "Well, if you complain about the school, I will put in a complaint against the LA."

"Do what you want to, but I know what I am going to be doing!" There was still an awful lot of looking around at each other, lots of red faces and nervous tapping of pens. They couldn't even meet my eye. The leader of the base said, "I did try."

"Yes, you did, and you worked very hard, but that doesn't right the fact that my son has been let down." The SEN Officer then said, "If we can't get him into school, then how can we give him the education?" It was at that point I reminded and made her familiar with my nugget of knowledge and quoted section 19 to her. Of course, she would have known it but chose not to make me aware of it in the past.

I added, "If I had kept my son in his bedroom for five years on purpose, I would have been put in prison years ago, no fines, no threats of nothing. It works both ways in my eyes, and I will make sure that someone is made accountable. I have rang or texted in every morning to report my son's absence as told to do." I then ended with, "I would like my son to have a home tutor in the interim time between schools." The SEN promised me that she would be on the case ASAP and assured me that things would be put in place very soon. And then she asked me, "Has that made you feel better, with me promising this will be done?"

"No, it hasn't. When it's on my table at home in black and white, then I will believe it. As far as I am concerned, my son has been out of sight, out of mind, and I have no faith in anyone anymore." I had never ever spoken out like this before, but I was determined to see this through for Charlie and to continue to fight for his rights and for him. For once, it wasn't me that ended up in tears in a meeting! During the meeting, my supporters in the room gave me the odd encouraging wink when I looked over at them. Afterwards, they said, "Well done, you did amazingly. I nearly jumped across the table to high-five you."

Since that meeting, and me finding my voice, it has made me much stronger in future meetings, but it's wrong that it had to come to that to spur me on. As soon as we got home, we sent an email to the MP. She was a great help and wrote letters to the Department of Education and asked us to keep her informed as to what was happening. Next on the agenda was the very complicated complaints procedure. Call me cynical, but I am sure that they make it more complicated than need be to deter people from continuing with it. But do it we did, listing all of the complaints that we had about each and every failing going back years. So I had the huge task of fishing out paperwork going back years, looking through old diaries, calendars, CAMHS and doctors' reports. Thank God I had saved them, as you will find out later that the LA and powers that be try and twist everything I said to save their skin.

So if ever you are in a similar situation, then keep everything, every email, every letter, text, even a phone call. Get the person's name and then follow it up with an email so that you leave a trail, as phone calls can't be proven. The response came back from our level one complaint, and it was a joke, blatantly trying their utmost to get out of things. So, I then escalated the complaint to level two. But to escalate, you have to go through the response from level one and state what and why you don't agree with the findings.

Once you can prove that, you can then move on to the next level, which we did, and again, they disagreed with us and our

90

outcomes of the last complaint. They were convincing, I must admit, all very plausible to an outsider looking in, and on paper, they had made it look like they had gone above and beyond. They like to blind you with big words and wording that is not at all easy to navigate. After level two couldn't be resolved, we could then legally go to the LGO (Local Government Ombudsman). All of this had very nearly fried my brain.

I was just a mum, not a solicitor, but I was absolutely determined to see this through for our lad Charlie. By all this time, it was months before it got to the LGO stage. I was very relieved when the ombudsman's investigator rang me as now she could take the reins. Kenny had been a fantastic help and support; he would read through paperwork to make sure I hadn't missed anything with my fine-tooth comb! Thank goodness for Kenny. All this had taken its toll on my mental health as apart from worrying about Charlie, I was now up against a big consortium, all of whom were sticking together and still trying to worm their way out. So, as you can imagine, when you are up against a big establishment, it is so exhausting, and you really do start to think, "Is this really what has happened?" or "Have I got the strength to keep this up?" But one look at Charlie, and I knew I would never give up!

CHAPTER NINE

In the interim, while awaiting the findings from the ombudsman, three home tutors were secured for Charlie. It still took almost half a term after I requested them in the meeting. Online teaching wouldn't have worked for Charlie as he responds much better face to face, as it keeps him focused and on track. Charlie had tutors for maths, English, and science. English and science were once a week each for one hour. Not much, I know, but we felt that was all Charlie could have coped with until his stamina had built up. The maths tutor would visit on a Monday morning for three hours. Her name was Marj, a very petite Jamaican lady in her sixties. She was very devoted and passionate about her work and would catch three buses to reach our home as she lived on the other side of the city. Now, three hours was a long time, but I certainly wasn't complaining as Charlie had waited so long for this. Also, it would have been a very long round trip for Marj for just an hour. We were just so very grateful to have her with us.

Charlie was getting really tired by the end of the three hours and was finding it so difficult to think. Marj was so enthusiastic about teaching Charlie and would say that he was a very bright boy. One Monday, Charlie refused to come down from his bedroom for his maths lesson, so Marj would go up to teach him in his bedroom. I would put a chair in his room for her with a cup of tea and a glass of water, and that is how she taught him from then on while she was with us, which was a few months. The only downside was that I had to sit in Charlie's bedroom as well with both of them, as understandably she wasn't allowed to be left in his bedroom unattended by a parent. So for three hours every Monday, we would head up there together, and my goodness, did that three hours drag.

Marj had a very soft, gentle Caribbean accent, which Charlie found incredibly hard to hear what she was saying. So, I would more or less have to keep repeating what Marj was saying to him. She had such a relaxing voice, one of those voices that you could just listen to all day, so relaxing in fact that I could quite easily have dozed off. The minute Marj would leave, Charlie would groan with exhaustion, hold his head, flop back onto his bed, and sleep. All of the tutors were very nice, and Charlie engaged well with them. All three tutors had to write a report at the end of each session to say how they thought Charlie had done during that lesson. They said the same: "Charlie engages well and is a lovely, polite, quiet student to teach and is capable of learning with help and support." The exact same thing that I had been saying for years! ... Hallelujah! All too soon, the tutors had to come to an end.

Now that Charlie was sixteen, we had to start looking for a suitable sixth form for him that he would feel comfortable with and, most importantly, meet his needs. No easy feat considering he had missed out on huge amounts of education, along with the fact he had not been able to take any GCSEs, of course, as he hadn't even been to school, let alone be able to learn anything in the short time that we had the tutors. But the LA said they wouldn't fund both the tutors and a setting that was appropriate.

One of the many things that Kenny and I found most upsetting was the fact that Charlie had missed out on taking his GCSEs. I know that they can be taken at any time of life, but it is such an important part of any teenager's life when they are growing up. The studying, ambition, shared revision with your mates, the nerves, the excitement of opening those all-important results with your friends or family, all the celebrating and supporting each other, choosing the next step and where to go, friendships, and the grand event at the end of every final year of school 'the proms.' Now, this was definitely a very low point for us both.

I loved seeing my friends' Facebook posts of their beautiful daughters in all their finery, looking so happy and excited, and all the boys looking just so grown up and handsome. The parents stood next to them, happy and smiling for the camera. They all looked so proud and happy. I hardly recognised some of the now young adults as they had all grown and changed so much. I still pictured them in my mind's eye as primary school-aged children, not as the young adults I saw before me now. It was so lovely to see, but my God, it tore at my heartstrings. I thought Charlie should be standing in that lineup with a smart suit on and maybe even a young lady on his arm to accompany him to the prom. It was just as if time had stood still in our house for the last six years or more. I just could not believe where all of those years had gone, and all of it spent trying to get our lovely boy an education... a human right, surely?

I couldn't hold my tears any longer and let them flow, letting all of my sorrow for Charlie out. I cried and cried. No way could I put this crying episode down to a sneezing fit! I feel grateful that we got to see Joseph in his smart suit with his beautiful girlfriend on his arm. They made a lovely couple and made us all very proud. Joseph had come out of this relatively unscathed, amazingly. He went through a couple of bad patches at secondary school, the general scraps that all lads have, chatting too much in class, and the odd silly behaviour in class. He had dyslexia and dyscalculia, which is a word and number blindness and also part of the umbrella on the autistic spectrum. Joseph was a really sociable young man, very friendly and keen to help people and kind-hearted.

Joseph got his chosen place at Oxford College and trained and qualified as a chef, something that he had always wanted to do. He had worked as a kitchen and food prep in our local village pub since he was fourteen, so he already had a fairly good knowledge of how a kitchen worked. We were all so proud of Joe, as, despite his learning difficulties and the pressure of what home life would some days be like, he did very, very well. He got a job as a chef in town and was there for almost two and a half years, but chafing is very unsociable hours. He had a change of heart and went back to college to do a carpentry course, disappointing as he was a talented chef, but as long as he was happy, that is the most important thing in life.

Sadly, by now, we had lost our border collie, Bonnie, having to have her put to sleep with, I suspect, cancer. Very sad, but I had always promised her that when her time came, I wouldn't let her suffer. After a few months, we really missed having a dog, something both Kenny and myself had always had growing up along with cats. So along came a very sweet, very mischievous whippet puppy who we called Fern, and what an absolute bundle of energy she was. She was a very cheeky pup, as they all are. When she wasn't having a mad moment of zoomies, she liked nothing better than to cuddle up next to you on the sofa. This had a positive effect on Charlie as she was the encouragement he needed to get him out of his bedroom, even if it was just for twenty minutes at a time. It was a vast improvement not to have him not coming out at all.

Fern was going through that chewing, teething stage and loved nothing more than to use our hands as a teething ring. Her teeth were like sharp little needles pricking at your skin, and it would hurt. We used to yelp at her like her mother and littermates would, to indicate how painful it was and quickly move our hand and replace it with one of her chewing toys. Charlie found all of this hilarious and seemed to enjoy the feeling of her teeth biting into him. It was a sensory thing, and the more he laughed, the more Fern enjoyed doing it. Her little tail was wagging, and her big brown eyes were as big as saucers with excitement. You couldn't help but laugh, and that is something I hadn't seen Charlie do in a very long time.

The healing powers of a dog are amazing. Fern is now three and has turned into the most loving, loyal, and funny dog you could wish for. If you are sad, she will come and sit next to you and either dab you with her wet nose or give you a lick. If Charlie is feeling grumpy or nervous, she will go up to him and pounce on him or just let him stroke her. Equally, if anyone is feeling poorly, she will happily snuggle up on the sofa with a blanket. A big plus is she gets me out once a day for a walk. Even on my lowest days, a walk outside seems to lift my mood, and nine times out of ten, you will see someone you know and have a little chat or a smile and a good morning.

Clair was still with us during this time, and once Fern had had all of her vaccinations, the three of us would take Fern out for a walk together to the local park. Charlie would hold her lead, and Fern would trot along by his side. This happened twice a week, and it was hoped that Charlie would carry it on in the future, which he did, albeit very occasionally. Clair's time was sadly coming to an end after her year with us, and she gave Charlie plenty of time to get used to the idea, as she understood that he hated goodbyes and had become very fond of Clair, we all had. She was a lovely person, so kind, understanding, and knowledgeable for such a young lady, and I am sure that she would have gone on from strength to strength within the mental health profession.

Before discharging Charlie, she wanted to make sure that another service and CAMHS would take Charlie on and continue with the work that she had been doing and to find another avenue to access education, as we haven't been able to find anywhere suitable, as all the special needs schools were miles away. Clair and I went to the CAMHS office. Charlie was supposed to come but wasn't up to it on the day. He felt very overwhelmed, with Clair leaving and entering the next stage of his life so up in the air. We met with the doctor who listened to both of us and was reading through his vast notes on Charlie. I really expressed to him how worried we all were and how we didn't want to feel on our own again. I needed help to be able to help Charlie. Yes, I cried yet again, as just going through it all really brings it home just what a terrible time Charlie has had. To see your child being sick with nerves, shaking, and on the point of passing out is just awful and made me, as his mum, feel helpless.

I told him all of this, and he seemed to be really understanding and said, "My word, Charlie has been let down, hasn't he?"

"Yes, he has," I just about managed to blub out. The doctor promised both Clair and myself that he would help us all and be a support for me, by way of ringing me once a week just to check I was doing ok and find ways to ease Charlie's anxieties. "I will also arrange a key worker from CAMHS to work directly with Charlie," he added. I felt myself sag with relief as I said, "God, what a huge relief to hear. Thank you, doctor." He was tapping his pen on his desk and smiled a thoughtful smile at me, and I said, "You really will help?"

"I promise," he said.

I would like to tell you at this point how wonderful and amazing he was, but I can't as I only met him once, and he only telephoned me twice. He never did meet Charlie, and I never saw him again, yet another empty promise! Clair had also arranged for Charlie and our family to be supported by the MASH (Multi-Agency Safeguarding Team) within the hub in our local town. We would have regular meetings called a TAF (Team Around the Family), and the locality worker would lead the meeting and help find ways to move forward and help Charlie. Alongside the meeting with the CAMHS doctor, we had a meeting with Charlie's new key worker in the hope that he could come up with some strategies or help navigate an alternative education setting rather than sixth form. Clair and I entered his small office and sat in the low foam armless chairs. It was a very sparse room with just a table in the middle with a box of tissues on it.

"I hope I don't need them again today," I remember thinking. He was pleasant enough, but he seemed overly positive in the sense of saying, "Charlie will be fine, don't worry," flailing his arms above his head, a very 'happy-go-lucky' attitude. I remember thinking, "I wish I had his faith." But once he had read all of his notes and had spoken to Chloe, he did come back down to earth. And although he was at a bit of a loss of where we went from here, he did have one suggestion, and that was that he knew of a man who had just recently moved to this area from London. He was working at the hub as part of the team of helpers of MASH. His area was something called EET (Education Employment Training), and they worked with young people aged sixteen to nineteen.

If you had that all-singing, all-dancing gold dust thing called an EHCP, it would be up until twenty-five. The help would entail Charlie accessing education or employment with support from the EET worker. So, of course, I was very keen as this sounded like just what Charlie needed. We were told that the EET worker was very experienced in autism and used to be an autism advisory teacher in a special needs school. He also had links and experience within the social service sector. The man from CAMHS seemed to think that if we were all in agreement, then this could be just what Charlie needed. Fortunately, we were all in agreement, so the referral was made. I was hanging onto this new development like I was hanging onto a sinking ship. And when CAMHS let me know a few weeks later that the referral had been accepted, I could have done a jig there and then. "Thank you so much," I gushed, so relieved that Charlie was going to get some help.

Now, I knew all this would take a while to sort out, so in the interim, I decided to do some more research for future sixth-form places. I seemed to have more zest in me now that I knew things were happening, and finding the right setting would tie in perfectly with the EET worker to help support the transition. In our town, there was an excellent special needs school with an exceptional reputation. "But did they have a sixth form?" I wondered. So, I rang them, and yes, they did have a sixth form. So I promptly made an appointment and was shown around by the headmaster, who was a lovely, kind man who listened, really listened as I explained to him about Charlie. I was honest and expressed that as he had been out of education and life in general for so long, getting Charlie into school was going to be no easy feat, and it would take a long time to re-engage him. Then, tentatively, almost too afraid to ask, "Do you have a place? And would you be able to meet Charlie's needs?" The head smiled and "Yes, we do have a place for Charlie and could meet his needs." I felt relief wash over me. He added, "We will have to dot a few I's and cross a few T's and, of course, put it to a panel to see if they agree."

"That's great, thank you," not wanting to get my hopes up.

Within a couple of weeks, the panel came back with a 'yes,' thank goodness. We were all very pleased indeed, including Charlie. I had a good feeling about this school and was quietly confident. This was going to be very challenging to get Charlie to this amazing school. The sixth form at the school concentrated on life skills, cooking a meal, using a washing machine, going shopping for ingredients to make a meal and handling money while shopping. Also, opportunities to go on short breaks and to the theatre or cinema, just perfect for what we were looking for Charlie. Now that the referral for the EET worker had gone through, we could start making plans for some transition work. But first, Charlie would have to get to know this new person. So, in the middle of December 2018, the EET worker and I spoke on the phone to arrange a first meeting. It was decided that as it was so close to the Christmas holidays, his first visit would be at the beginning of January 2019 after the schools had started back. I then went up and explained the plan to Charlie. He nodded and smiled, "Ok, Mum." We all felt like a weight had been lifted that Christmas

CHAPTER TEN

Early January arrived, and Peter came for his first home visit. Initially, it was just for a general chat, so there was no pressure on Charlie if he couldn't come down to meet him this first time. He didn't want to come downstairs, which was understandable after another fairly long gap of not seeing anyone.

We sat down and went through Charlie's background, which he seemed mostly unaware of. He was very shocked at how much schooling Charlie had missed out on. I told him as much as I could cram into the hour that we had. He seemed equally surprised when I went through Charlie's sensory issues, how he would only wear shorts and a T-shirt regardless of the weather, and that he found making eye contact very difficult, not due to rudeness but due to being part of his autism.

Peter looked at me totally agog, with his mouth open and shaking his head, saying, "No, really?" Not knowing how to answer this, I just replied, "Well, yes, it's all part and parcel of being autistic," still shaking his head, "Oh, right. Okay." I thought, "Crikey, I would have thought that he would have known that, being an expert. He must have come across this before." So, I braved it and asked him, "In your experience, have you ever come across other students who were too anxious to attend school?" I wish I hadn't asked, for his reply was, "No, not for this long. We would always be honest with the parent about problem-solving, and if we didn't think it was the right school, then we would tell them so." This didn't really enthuse me with optimism, but I thought, "Well, he must know what he's on about to have worked in such positions." I tried to put it to the back of my mind, as I didn't need anything else to go wrong. "Think positive,

Sharon," I kept telling myself. After all, he had worked in a lot of SEN schools in London.

The next meeting was arranged for the following week, and this time, Charlie came downstairs all ready to meet Peter. We waited and waited. I just about managed to keep Charlie downstairs until he arrived almost an hour later. I know that these things happen and cannot always be helped, but trying to explain that to Charlie was no easy feat. Like with so many autistics, time, and structure are very important, almost obsessively so. If you said eleven, it would have to be eleven; no room for movement. So every second past eleven seemed like an hour to him... and me too! As all this was so stressful, thinking any minute now he was going to retreat back upstairs, I always explained that sometimes lateness couldn't be avoided, especially in the line of work that professionals had. But in Charlie's black-or-white world, there is no room for any grey areas whatsoever. Charlie did stay downstairs, thank goodness. When Peter arrived, I guided them both toward the dining room table to sit there. Fern was still a young, bouncy whippet and would get very excited when anyone came, and I didn't want Peter getting jumped all over by her if they were to sit on the sofa. So once they were settled at the table and the dog was semi-under control, I left them to it. I didn't want them to feel as though I was interfering, and it would be good for them to get to know each other a little better. I was only in the kitchen, so Peter could ask me anything if he wasn't sure. I got on with some jobs, peeling veg ready for dinner that night, and made Kenny's and Joseph's sandwiches for work the next day, that sort of thing to busy myself.

They were getting on well, from what I could hear, playing a game. Then Peter was starting to do a star chart with Charlie to try and determine what makes him more anxious and strategies to help lessen them. All went well, and we arranged the next week's visit. That's pretty much how it continued over the next couple of months, slowly building a rapport together. Still, the odd lateness now and again, but we resolved this by changing the day for a less busy one for Peter, as he suggested that would suit him better. We were fine with that, not like we were going anywhere!

So, all was going well, and early March arrived. I was invited to a TAF meeting (Team Around the Family) organised by my support worker from the hub. Present in the meeting were Peter, a support worker, SEN Officer from the county council, and myself. The meeting started well with all the usual introductions. Then Charlie's SEN Officer started saying, "We need to get Charlie into this school or that school, which would be just ideal for him." I tried to say that he had already got a place in a lovely SEN school and couldn't possibly go to any other as they were all miles away. Still, they seemed to be all talking at once about what they thought would be best for my son.

I couldn't get a word in edgeways, or so it felt. "We have tried schools further afield, and he won't go," I just about managed to blurt out, followed by, "It would be like setting him up for another fall." The SEN still kept mentioning other schools and that maybe they would work out cheaper for the county; I don't know. With all this talking about what they thought would or wouldn't work, I was beginning to feel like I might as well not have been there. I'm sure that it wasn't intended, but that's how I felt. Suddenly, it was like I couldn't hear anything, only mouths opening and closing, and my eyes misting over with tears. I just wanted to be heard. The next thing, I am gently tapping on the table with the palm of my hand, "Please, please, he won't go. I just know he won't go." I sobbed and sobbed. The support worker and SEN Officer were very kind and understanding, and that's when the SEN Officer realised just how awful things had become. The desperation in my voice spoke volumes.

I really hate crying or showing my emotions to anyone, let alone a roomful of practical strangers. So, it was decided that Peter would undertake the role of supporting Charlie to reintegrate him into school. My shoulders physically sagged with relief, along with tears of utter relief and hope.

It was later that afternoon that I told Charlie the good news. I decided to take a walk with Fern. It had been quite a morning, and I needed to clear this headache from all the tension. I hadn't been out long when I heard my phone buzz, indicating I had a text message. It was from Peter, "How are you? I didn't like seeing you upset earlier. I think you are one pretty amazing woman."

"How kind of him," I thought and texted back, "I'm fine, thanks. Sometimes, it all just gets a bit much to deal with." And that was that.

The next week, Peter visited as arranged, and Charlie was still getting ready. If something hadn't gone right the first time for him, either his hair hadn't laid flat, or he couldn't get his sock on comfortably, so inevitably, it would upset the whole process. But he was coming down, and that was the main thing. I always got a feeling that he just wasn't the way he would act beforehand, like not getting out of bed or more subtle things like his paleness or his extra quietness the day before. So, the fact that Charlie had showered and dressed was a good sign despite his bad start. While we waited for Charlie to finish getting ready to come down, Peter and I sat at the table and just had a general chit-chat to pass the time. I had a lot of paperwork out on the table as I had recently signed up for a two-year course in spiritual healing with one of my good friends, Liz.

We were both debating whether or not to do it but decided that we would and that we could always help each other. I also thought that now things had started to look up for Charlie, it would be nice for me to get out once a fortnight and have a change of scene and learn something new. Kenny was really pleased and keen for me to do it and agreed it would do me good. And just maybe, I thought that if I felt a bit better mentally and had something else to focus on, it would benefit all of us, especially Charlie, as we were both trying something new. I could show him that even though it was daunting and I was nervous about doing the course, I was going to give it a good go.

So when Peter wanted to know all about it, I was only too pleased to tell him what I was doing. The first thing we learned was the chakras, the names, and the colors of them. Peter said that he was familiar with that sort of thing as that is where his roots are from. We chatted some more about it. Then I noticed that he was acting a bit nervous himself, fiddling with his wedding ring so much so that it flew off his finger across the table. He was then fiddling with his mobile and accidentally rang his boss. I didn't think too much of it as it was maybe a nervous habit he had.

Charlie eventually came downstairs, and I left them to their session as normal. After arranging the next week's visit, I said goodbye. That evening, Kenny and I were going on a rare night out with some friends, something that we tried to do every few weeks or so. This particular night there were ourselves and three other couples from the village all going to the village social club for a function. My mum and Joe would be at home, so Charlie was in very safe hands. Both lads quite liked it when we went out for the evening as I always brought them some treats, crisps and chocolate being a firm favourite. Charlie was more than happy munching them in his room playing on his computer, and Joe very often stayed downstairs with his Nan watching telly or a film. We were only down the lane where the clubhouse was, so if anything should happen, we could be home within minutes.

At around ten thirty, I heard my phone buzz and looked at it immediately, worried it was Mum or Joe. But it was from Peter, strange, I thought. I wonder what he wants at this time of night. The message read, "How are you? xx." I thought, why is he putting kisses, but nevertheless, I texted back, "I'm fine, thanks. You?" I didn't know what to put. His reply came back rapidly, "Thinking about you, Sharon. xx."

"I'm fine, don't worry about me. There are plenty of people a lot worse off. xx." I put kisses back, as I didn't want him to think that I was being offish. Also, it wasn't unknown in the past for other helpers that we've had to sign off with kisses, although never from a man, I naively thought. But then I reasoned that with Peter coming from London, maybe people were more open and friendly there. God, how absolutely stupid do I feel about thinking that way now. Gullible me

I still didn't think anything of it. I was more worried that I had worried him enough to make him text me. I must have worried him from all that crying I did in the meeting.

The next week rolled around, and all went well with Peter and Charlie. The week after that, not so well! I could not persuade Charlie to come downstairs at all. His hair was sticking up all over the place, and he had got himself in a proper temper over it. I tried to calm the situation and make light of it by saying, "It's fine. I can soon wet it down for you." He had washed his hair earlier and then put his headphones on, so he had a big ridge in his hairline and had got to the point of no return. It was going to be a big no for today's visit.

I felt instantly stressed, worried that Peter would be cross as I hadn't managed to persuade Charlie. I had this thing that I hated letting anyone down and that nobody would believe how hard I was trying with Charlie. I was panicking and worried.

I need not have worried, though, as Peter was very good about it and said, "Don't worry, as these things happen. We can have a catch-up instead." We did and talked about how Charlie had been in the week, which wasn't great, but I didn't elaborate on this as it was nothing major; just been a tough week. Just as he was leaving, he looked at me and said, "You know, Sharon, everything will be okay." I was holding things together up until that point, as at the time I was still very low. So, if anyone showed me the slightest bit of kindness, it would often start me crying again. I could, as predicted, feel the threat of a tear spilling over my lower lid, so I took a tissue to wipe it away quickly. Smiling through, I said, "Yes, I really hope so." With that, he held out his arms. "Come here and give me a cuddle," he ordered. "No, I will be okay." Grabbing for another tissue, he still persisted with outstretched arms heading my way. "Come on, come on," he repeated, so I did and let him give me a cuddle. Again, nothing too unusual about that, I thought; many other professionals had given me a hug on the many occasions I had not been able to hold back my tears. He continued to text me during the next week, always signing off with kisses.

The next week, I felt much more myself as I had had a good week with Charlie. We had walked Fern to the village shop, and that was such a huge step for Charlie, and I clung to any step forward. When Peter visited that week, I told him how well things had been. I left them as normal to do their work, and the hour soon passed. As Peter walked down the hall to leave, he had just got to the front door and then turned to me. "Give me a cuddle," he demanded. "No, I am fine this week. Things have gone well; I'm not upset," I said. Still, he persisted. "Come on, come here," so as not wanting to appear rude, I gave him a hug. That's when I felt him push himself up against my groin area. I felt embarrassed, but again, I didn't think it was done on purpose, even though it did feel a bit close for comfort. The texts still continued, giving subtle compliments that were something or nothing and could be taken either way, always bolstering me up and saying how well I was doing, being supportive... or so I thought

Charlie wouldn't come out of his room the next week, so I was very up and down again. But again, Peter said, "Don't worry, as actually, I can't stay for long today as I've been called to an emergency meeting for one of the young people I support."

"You should have cancelled us; we would have understood," I said, feeling even more guilty for him being here and Charlie not coming out of his room. "I like seeing you, Sharon, and to have a chat," he said. After about twenty minutes, we made the usual arrangements for the next week's visit, and he left. Half an hour had passed, and I had a text from him. "My meeting has finished earlier than expected, so I can come back round, and we can talk some more if you like. xx" My reply was, "No, that's fine; you will get sick of hearing about it all." I was referring to all the upset and worry my family was going through regarding my complaint. "It will do you good to talk about it. I don't mind listening and helping you at all."

"Okay, thanks. If you have time, that's really kind of you." He soon arrived back at my home. Now, every single time he has visited, I have always directed him to the table due to the pup, so I thought it strange that this time, when he came in, he sat down on the sofa and tapped the place next to him, indicating for me to sit next to him. "Sit down here," reinforcing his tapping instruction, so I did, and my god do I wish now that I hadn't, as this was going to be the start of my worst nightmare and one that

I will never fully get over. I didn't know it on this occasion, though, as it happened very cleverly over time.

As soon as we sat down together, he asked, "Would you like to see a picture of my son?"

"That would be nice. Okay." So off he went out to his car to get his private phone. I would imagine he showed me his toddler son dancing, kicking a ball, innocent enough. I thought that he was being friendly. He then said kindly, "You know, Sharon, if ever you need anyone to talk to, I'm here for you." While he said this to me, at the same time, he put his hand on my knee and squeezed it. "Thank you," I said, feeling grateful that I had such an understanding person helping my family. He repeated those same words two more times, offering me a listening ear if ever I needed it, and each time he said it, his hand moved further and further up my leg and moved towards my inner thigh. "That's really kind of you, Peter, but I would have to be in real dire straits to bother you or my support worker; you are all so busy. I will be okay."

"Honestly, I am fine." Without saying another word, he pulled me over towards him with his arm and was cuddling me tightly. I was by now in a semi-laid position across him and couldn't feel as though I could move. I stayed still for a few seconds, thinking, "What am I going to do?" So, I slowly started lifting myself back up into a sitting position. That's when he touched my chin, lifted my head, kissed me, and started touching my breasts. I didn't know what to do; I couldn't think straight. I pulled away and asked what was going on. "I'm sorry, Sharon; I can't help it as I have feelings for you and feel a strong connection. I think it's your spiritual side and my roots. I just wanted to get up off the sofa. I don't know what to do or say to you about this." I now know exactly what I should have said to him, but at the time, I didn't. I had never been in a situation like this before and didn't know what was going on. I certainly didn't know at the time that it was the start of him grooming me.

Later that same afternoon, he texted me, "Are you okay, Sharon? I am sorry. Sometimes, I am a typical man and get carried away. I can't help these feelings I have. When I touch your arm, a sensation goes through me, and I can't explain it."

"Oh god," I inwardly thought. I was panicking and did not need this on top of everything else. I didn't know what to do, so I did nothing. Shortly after this happened, he was going to be away in another country to visit family for three weeks, so I was hoping that by the time he got back, he would have realised that this was just some fleeting crush and he could get back on track with helping my son.

All the time he was away, I kept thinking, how on earth am I going to act as if nothing had happened and be normal with him? After his revelation, my brain was all but frazzled by now, what with everything else going on, and I could well do without it.

Charlie had slipped back and started to isolate in his bedroom again as he couldn't see the point of coming out of his room if he wasn't going anywhere. "How about we walk Fern and go to the shop?" I encouraged, but the answer was always the same, "No." He had found a new online game and was playing with some online friends that we didn't know. They all seemed to be getting on well and seemed friendly. In fact, it was nice to hear Charlie interacting with others. He always felt safe behind the screen of his computer and would speak a bit more. He had two regular gamers that he would play with, and we knew the family well, so we never had any issues

On the third week of Peter being away, I was preparing Charlie for his return. I so wanted Charlie to start coming down again, more so than ever now. It was late Sunday evening, around eleven thirty, when I received a message from a name I did not know. It was one of the gamers' dads; he wanted to make me aware that Charlie was being very abusive and had destroyed his son's virtual dinosaur nest. I was mortified on hearing this and reassured the man that both my husband and I would be dealing with it immediately, which we did there and then. We were really cross with him for being abusive and explained how careful you have to be online, with the added threat of "Any more of that, and we will stop you playing that game," which we knew would usually be enough to get him back in line. Thinking that was the end of it, I then received two other messages from two other men in their early twenties, saying that Charlie was also threatening them, swearing, and destroying their base. Again, I apologised profusely and told them to report and block Charlie to put an end to it once and for all

Then, the first man messaged me again. By this time, it was gone midnight. He showed me a screenshot of what Charlie had been saying. Charlie had invited all three lads to our house for a fight, and Charlie was going to take all three of them on. If that wasn't bad enough, he gave out our address and postcode just to make sure they could find us

These lads accepted the invitation and told Charlie that they were going to get in the car and travel down from Nottingham and fight him. I was terrified, and my arms and legs went numb and then to jelly. We went mad at Charlie; how on earth had made him do such a stupid thing? He wasn't a bit worried, though. "Don't worry, Mum, they won't come; it's all talk." I wasn't taking any chances, so for the rest of Sunday into Monday, I stayed downstairs wide awake, waiting for any sign of these men. I was still spooked by morning and felt sick and really wobbly. The men were still messaging me, "If Charlie doesn't stop swearing, we are paying a visit." They threatened. I had never been so scared. Joseph blocked them for me so that they couldn't contact me anymore, and I told Charlie I was so frightened that I was going to call the police. He went berserk at me, saying that they would arrest him. "Not you, Charlie, they would help us," I reasoned.

Thank goodness all went quiet, but all the same, I continued to stay downstairs for the Monday into Tuesday and the Tuesday into Wednesday, still not having slept. I was just too worried to go to sleep in case they pulled up outside in the dead of night. I had to be aware so that I could act quickly and call the police; Kenny and Joe thought I was mad.

I couldn't cope much more; I had the ombudsman to contend with, along with trying to get Charlie into his new school. Just to top things off, through the post that morning, I had the dreaded PIP form (Personal Independence Payment) to start filling out on Charlie's behalf, as now that he was sixteen, he had to transfer from DLA (Disability Living Allowance). Now, anyone who has ever had to fill these forms in will know just what a task it is, let alone trying to persuade Charlie to attend the face-to-face assessment that would also loom upon us once the forms had been filled in. I prayed that we could get him to go, as you only get two chances to cancel then the claim is stopped, and the whole thing has to restart from the beginning. I was just trying to get my mind in some sort of unmuddled thought when the phone thrilled me from my thoughts. "Who's that now?" I thought.

It was more hassle for me to try and contend with; the phone call was from the county council informing me that Charlie's transport application had been turned down! The reason? Because now that he had turned sixteen, transport was much more difficult to qualify for. The other reason was that as the journey was barely two miles, they thought he could walk! My god, what next? What do I do now? There was no way he could walk as he would have to navigate two very busy roads and a bypass, added to that his hypermobility and autism, let alone his anxiety. Obviously, once you reach sixteen, all your ailments vanish, and all is good. "That is why he is going to be going to a special needs school," I tried to explain to the sickeningly calm woman on the other end of the phone when I rang the council back, but to no avail. I would have to take it to appeal. So, of course, that's what I did. Just that, more paperwork, more chasing doctors and nurses for proof of what I was saying was true, equalled more stress. I felt like I had not a soul that I could call upon for help; my friends, of course, would have helped me in a heartbeat, as they have told me since, but me being me, I didn't want to be a burden to any of them. After all, everyone has their problems and dilemmas.

I was surviving on autopilot. Just. At the time, I didn't realise it, but I was extremely depressed. I say I didn't realise it, as it had crept up on me very slowly over the years. I was blinded by the all-consuming fight after fight that was endured for so many years. Looking back now, I think I just got used to feeling so low and thought that was normal, and that's how it was. We were so isolated; I really felt like I had no one, and forever putting on that brave face was so tiring. If anyone saw me in the village shop or even my own family and friends, they would never be able to tell that not ten minutes before, I would be a crumpled crying mess on the floor. I could hide things well for the sake of Kenny and my mum. If I felt things getting too much, I would say to Kenny, "Just nipping to the loo."

"Okay," he would innocently reply, not having any idea that I was having a sob, a quick wipe over my face with a flannel and a bit of compact powder and a smile; no one was any the wiser.

I was clinging to the fact that Peter would be back any day; he would know what to do, surely?

CHAPTER ELEVEN

On Wednesday morning, I received a text from Peter saying that he was back from his three-week leave and wanted to visit for a catch-up, as he had heard the good news that I had secured Charlie a place at the special needs school. So, of course, I wanted to see him and tell him all about the other obstacles that had been encountered since he had been away.

So when the doorbell rang later that day, I was feeling relieved to at last be able to share what had been going on. I was sure he would know what to do about the transport appeal and could hopefully write me a backup letter for extra evidence. I was also going to tell him about these threats that I had been getting and was hoping that he could then reinforce to Charlie what we had also said about the dangers of the internet, etc. Now that Charlie definitely had his school place, we could start planning when the transition work would start.

I started telling him all about what had been going on, and he said, "You look stressed."

"I am," I replied, shaking at the very thought of all I had to do. So when he said, "God, I've missed you, come here," holding both his arms out, indicating a comforting hug, I did. He kept repeating, "I've missed you, I've missed you," whilst kissing me. By this time, my brain had hit overload. I wanted advice and help from this man. I didn't know what to do as his hands were all over my body. It was then that he sexually assaulted me, bearing down on me, saying, "Relax, just relax." He kept on saying. The pain was incredible, like shards of glass cutting into me. I could feel the pain but felt totally numb in my mind and not thinking anything at all. I had shut down like it wasn't happening to me. How can it be? This isn't my body! Something that haunts me to this day; the specialists call it fight, flight, or freeze.

When it was over, he asked to use the bathroom; I nodded and said, "Yes." He was gone for ages, and when he came back to the living room, I was visibly shaking. He kissed the top of my head, "I have to go back to work now. See you at the TAF meeting on Friday." Then he was gone. What had just happened to me? I thought he liked me, I liked him, I trusted him, he had always been so kind and said all the right things, and I generally thought he was a genuine, sincere person.

I was in shock and still not fully aware of the seriousness of what had just happened, and it still felt very surreal. I was in the most awful pain, so I somehow got upstairs and slowly lowered myself into the warm water, gritting my teeth with the burning pain. While I lay there, it suddenly hit me like a ton of bricks. My Charlie was only upstairs in his bedroom. The brazenness of this man, the confidence he must have had just knowing that he wouldn't come down. I sat in the bath, just staring into nothingness for what seemed a very long time. I had to pull myself together, though, as Joseph was due home from work soon, and my mum would be back after meeting her friend for lunch. I could never tell anyone about this; after all, who would believe a depressed, always-crying mother over a professional? About an hour after he left, he sent me a text with the following. "I'm sorry, Sharon, about what happened; I feel really guilty. I hope that we can still get along and it won't affect my work with Charlie." I didn't reply; I felt sick to my core. I don't know how I did it, but somehow nobody noticed how upset I was, as by now, I was somewhat of an expert in hiding how I really felt to my family and close friends.

Two days later, it was Friday and the morning of the TAF meeting. I so much wanted to cancel the meeting so that I wouldn't have to see him, but I had to be strong and keep Charlie in the forefront of my mind, as this was going to be the meeting that would set out strategies for how to support Charlie getting into school. "I can't not go; I'd fought so hard. Think of Charlie." I kept repeating in my head like a mantra. I was still very sore and had now developed a dull ache in my side, just below my ribs in the soft fleshy flank area. I took some paracetamol and got on the bus for the journey into town. I arrived at the hub, which is a huge, almost Victorian-looking building with a large horseshoe courtyard in the centre. Today, it looked even more imposing than normal.

I was shaking like a leaf as I entered the hub reception area. The receptionist smiled, "Can I help you?"

"Yes, thank you. I am here for a meeting with the locality worker (support worker)." I couldn't even speak his name. I was asked to take a seat while the receptionist rang through to another room, I guess to let them know of my arrival. I was really, really dreading this, and every second that passed seemed like an eternity. I could hear footsteps outside coming nearer and nearer from the courtyard. Then the door opened, and it was him, "Hello, Sharon. How are you?" he said as cool as a cucumber as if this were the most natural thing in the world to him.

He was smiling and acting his usual self. My reaction was that I just looked blankly at him and just managed to say, "Okay."

"Follow me, Sharon, and we will go over to the meeting room and start." Just before we entered the room on the other side of the building, he stopped and took my arm to pull me back, and he said, "I am sorry, Sharon; I did not mean to hurt you." I said nothing; I couldn't. I was rendered dumb. Looking back now, I strongly believe that he only said sorry as he was probably worried that I would break down in the meeting and tell my support worker everything. God, I wish I had known, but he was extremely clever and knew full well that I was good at hiding things and that I hated making a fuss, especially worrying my family; he had it all worked out. The meeting soon got underway, with the opening line from the support worker being, "You will be very pleased to hear,

Sharon, that Peter can continue to support Charlie until just after the September holidays." She was naturally over the moon with this announcement, as she knew how hard things had been for us all these years. I, as you can imagine, on the other hand, was not over the moon. Considering this was April, I wasn't sure that I could hold things together for another five months.

After this announcement, I had no idea what else was said; I just couldn't think. He was just looking at me, smiling as if I would be pleased. It wasn't until a week later when the notes from the meeting were sent to me, that I was able to read through it. The very sight of his name in print made me shake, and to think I had to see him and, worse still, let him into my home. The only thing that kept me going was thinking, "Come on, Sharon, just get over these few months, and Charlie will be in school at long last, and you never have to set eyes on him again."

By now, the dull ache in my side was getting worse, more like a ball of burning fire. I was putting ice packs on the area and taking regular pain relief, but I was in agony, and I had started feeling unwell in myself too. My hands and feet were always icy cold; I had a permanent headache and was feeling trembly. I tried to struggle on until one Saturday morning when the pain was just unbearable, and I was feeling more ill by the hour. Our doctors were closed for the weekend, so I rang the out-of-hours number and got an appointment with a locum doctor on call at the local cottage hospital. Kenny took me, looking very worried about what could be causing all this discomfort.

The doctor called me into her consulting room, asked me some questions, asked me to lie on the examination couch and gave me a full examination. She took some blood and a urine sample. After the examination, she asked me to get dressed and come and take a seat at her desk. "Is everything okay?" she asked me kindly. "I'm fine, thank you," was my parrot fashion reply.

"Are you sure that there is nothing you want to tell me? Or has something happened to you to make you have this pain?"

"No, nothing, doctor. What's wrong with me?" I am getting worried now.

"You have a very nasty kidney infection, so you will need a strong course of antibiotics, and if you get no better within 48 hours, I will need to see you again."

"Okay" was all I could muster. The doctor asked me some more personal questions, and I still don't know to this day if she could tell something had happened. I had lost so much weight and went down to 7 stone, and I looked worn out. Still, she said, "You know you can tell me."

"No, honestly, I'm fine," I replied, praying that I sounded more convincing than I felt. I soon started to feel better as the tablets began to work, although I did need a second course as the infection had not quite cleared up.

The next few weeks were horrendous, having to see him still, and now it was twice a week instead of once to have more consistency for Charlie. The first visit after the meeting was one of the worst, as he was just trying to normalise what had happened. "Hi, how's things going?" he smiled that first time.

"Been better," I said coldly and angrily. My confusion about what had happened was clearing, and now it was being replaced with anger. He must have sensed it because, after a while, he apologised again, "I am really sorry, Sharon, but I have feelings for you, very strong feelings." Then he stepped toward me and hugged me again and was trying to kiss me, saying, "I can feel a connection when I touch your arm." I turned away from him, and he stopped.

The other time he tried it on was when I was having a huge task getting Charlie to come downstairs. He could see I was crying and struggling, and yet he still tried to touch me and was saying all these things to me. I went into the hallway and called up to Charlie to "please come down." It had been arranged by Charlie and 'him' that as a treat for going to school for a short while, they would go for a milkshake in town.

Of course, Charlie would only go if I did. Charlie eventually came down, so off we set for the cafe. We stayed for about half an hour, the longest half an hour of my life. 'He' sat directly opposite me and kept staring at me. I hated the fact I had to be all nice and pleasant to this man who had groomed me and, I now know, sexually assaulted me. I say now know, as I still wasn't sure if he did at the time, as I didn't say no, and I didn't say yes. Of course, now I know that's exactly what he did to me, a very clever man who made me trust him as he knew I was very vulnerable, and he took total advantage of the fact.

When we arrived back home, Charlie wanted to show him something that he had done, so he had to come into our home. He only stayed a few minutes, and when I showed him to the front door, he turned to me, "Let's go upstairs."

"No way," I said, "Okay, but you've got me all riled up." He grinned at me. He was blatant and did not care one bit that Charlie was sitting on his own in the living room waiting for me! What was wrong with this man? I could not take much more.

By now, it was early June, and I was not well at all. My weight had now gone down to six and a half stone; I couldn't eat or sleep. One morning, I was in the shower washing my hair when I noticed that the water wasn't draining away down the plughole, and the water was above my ankles. I soon discovered the cause; my hair was falling out, and big clumps had blocked the plughole. I know everyone loses hair once in a while, but I've never lost this much.

When the same thing kept on happening every time I washed my hair, I got really worried. What was happening to me? I fretted.

I was in a constant state of distress but still had to shield my family from what had gone on. I was in such a muddle I wasn't even sure what had happened. I would walk endlessly for miles over the fields with Fern, where I knew not a soul would be, and I would cry and sob as loud as I liked, saying, "Please, please help me, anybody, help me." I would cry that much I couldn't see where I was walking; poor Fern would look up at me with her big soulful eyes wondering what was wrong with me. I literally felt that I was going to end up doing something awful to myself unintentionally, like stepping out into the road, as my mind was so mushed I couldn't think straight at all. I now knew it was time to seek help from my doctor. I literally felt that I was going to end up doing something awful to myself unintentionally, like stepping out into the road, as my mind was so mushed I couldn't think straight at all.

Twice, when I was in a large supermarket in town, I was pushing the trolley, and all of a sudden, I had no idea where I was, how I got there and, more frighteningly, how I was going to get home. I shut my eyes, trying not to slide to the floor as everything seemed far away. I thought I was going to faint, and I held onto the trolley tightly until slowly, my bearings started to come back. Looking back now, it was more than likely a panic attack; it was so distressing. I now knew it was time to seek help from my doctor.

CHAPTER TWELVE

Sat in the waiting room of the doctor's surgery on that sunny June morning, I was feeling less than sunny, and this was the one time I hoped the doctor would be running late. I looked around the waiting room, observing all the people coming and going. I wished for a foot sprain or earache, anything other than this overwhelming feeling of sadness. How could I explain all this in a ten-minute appointment? Where do I start? The more I sat and thought, the more tears threatened to appear. I stared into space, trying not to blink, as if blinking would make the tears spill down my face. The stinging and smarting of not blinking overtook me, so I quickly leaned over to the table in the middle of the seats where I was sitting. It had the usual array of Good Housekeeping, Take a Break, and Country Life. I grabbed the nearest one and held it up close to my face to hide the tears. The last thing I needed was some caring soul to see me or, worse still, ask how I was and what was wrong!

Soon enough, I heard my name over the intercom system instructing me which room to go to.

"God, Sharon, this is it now or never," I thought to myself nervously as I made my way down the long corridor to the doctor's room. How I wished the corridor could have gone on for miles to give me just a bit more time. It wouldn't have made any difference, though, looking back, as my mind was muddled and overloaded with stress and worry. There would never have been enough time.

I knocked on her door gingerly. "Come in and take a seat," the doctor said cheerfully, indicating with her hand where to sit. Then she turned to me and smiled. "What can I do for you?" I couldn't speak! This was not how I wanted it to be. But try as I might, I felt like I had a lump the size of a melon stuck in my throat as I desperately fought back the tears. But it was no use, as the tears quickly turned into big, gulping sobs. I wanted to come across as a capable mum who was coping, not a blithering wreck! Who was I kidding?

The doctor gently said, "Take your time," handing me a box of tissues. She had the kindest, most genuine smile, making me cry even more. I had held all this in for years, and now I feared I would be unable to stop. Once I had managed to semi-compose myself, I explained to her the years and years of my poor son's anxiety and school refusals, how isolated he was in his bedroom all the time, how isolated we all were, and how much it impacted our family. The doctor would have known much of this, as CAMHS would have copied her into any care plans and medication changes. But I guess, having never gone to her myself, she wasn't to know just how difficult things had become over the years. Charlie would never have been able to visit the doctors unless he was really poorly with a chest infection or similar.

I told her how I felt nothing but misery and utter despair, feeling like I was going to go mad or my head would explode. The lovely doctor continued to listen tentatively, and then I blurted out, "A man who was supposed to be helping my son and me has done something to me that was not very nice." I will always remember those words and the sheer emotion that went with them. I broke down again, almost being sick with all the crying. "Was he a family friend who was helping you?"

"No, he was a helper that CAMHS and the county council sent," I replied.

"Where is he from?" Her face had now changed to a serious one.

"He came from London a few months back but relocated to Bicester." Then came the question I knew she would ask, but it was one that I was dreading all the same. "What did he do to you?" I told her all about the kind words, the texts, then asking me for cuddles, then it progressed to kissing, and him telling me he had feelings for me, and that awful, painful afternoon back in April. I sobbed to her, "Why would he do that to me?"

"Because he groomed you and slowly built up trust with you; then it very much sounds like he forced himself on you."

"Oh no, I am not sure what happened, doctor. I didn't say no; I didn't say yes. It was all such a blur, and I lost a sense of all reality and went numb."

"The very fact he had to tell you to relax tells me differently," she said softly.

Her tone then changed again. "What's his name?"

"What's the name of his boss?"

"Contact number for the council?" I said, "Why, doctor?"

"Because I will have to report this man."

"Oh god no, please, please no, don't," I begged and begged her. She explained that she had a legal obligation to report this behaviour and what he had done to me. As he was in a position of power and trust and a professional, it would have been made very clear to him in his training that this sort of abuse of power is wrong, and under no circumstances will he be allowed to work with children or vulnerable adults again.

"Please don't do, doctor," I said desperately again. "I don't want him to lose his job as he might have been sincere, as he told me on two or three occasions that sometimes he gets carried away and said he is a typical man." I was in total utter denial of what he had done to me and feel extremely gullible and naive now that I am in a much better place that I couldn't even comprehend thinking that way. But I take some solace in the fact that when you are in the depths of such depression and pure exhaustion, thinking straight is near impossible. The doctor was busily tapping away on her computer all the time, asking me more questions. "But he was such a nice man, doctor, and so convincing," I tried to justify my gullibility for not seeing him for what he was.

"Yes, he was more than likely a professional groomer and very good at it too," she added. "But I always thought that I was a good judge of character."

"He was an expert, Sharon, and at how quickly he did it to you in just a few weeks/months back, that theory backs up that he has done it before."

"But why did he do it to me? Especially when he knew and could see what a dreadful state I was in," trying to put things into some sort of perspective.

"That's why he did it, Sharon, because you are vulnerable and so low. It was easier for him to take advantage of you; that's how groomers work."

"But honestly, doctor, I thought he was okay, and he is helping Charlie and seems so nice." The doctor's no-nonsense reply summed it up. "That's what they used to say about Jimmy Saville," followed by, "Sharon, I wish you had come to me sooner when all this first happened. It must have been horrendous for you having to still see him."

"I wish I had as well now, but I thought if I could just stick it out for a few months until he had got Charlie into school, I could then try and get over it. But I couldn't face another day of seeing him and having him in my house as if nothing had happened."

From there on in, things moved very fast, and I honestly don't know how I would have coped without my GP. She rang me every day for about a week, supporting me and helping me. She gave me a phone number for a local sexual abuse centre where I could arrange some counselling.

I rang my support worker to tell her that I didn't want 'him' visiting my family anymore. The doctor had explained to me that she had to let my support worker know what had been going on but couldn't tell her my name due to patient confidentiality. I plucked up the courage and rang her. I was very upset, and she kindly arranged to come and visit me. She was also very supportive, and she asked to see the texts he had sent me. I showed her, and she took them off of my phone to stop me from getting upset if I ever looked at them again. They could also be used as proof. I asked her where they were going to be stored in case I ever needed them in the future. "They will be held with HR at the county council," she told me.

The next day, I was informed that 'he' had been suspended with immediate effect and that they had taken away his laptop and mobile phone. He was told under no circumstances was he to try to make contact with me (which he did!). There was to be an enquiry and then an internal disciplinary hearing to see if he would lose his job. All of this took two months in total, the longest time to have to wait.

While all this was going on, I won the appeal for the taxi transport, so I was able to take Charlie to school and then walk back. Again, it was decided that to start with, it would only be for very short periods of time, one hour to start with – ideal. They were going to be going at Charlie's pace and would not push him into anything at all that he didn't feel comfortable with, which totally took the pressure off of all of us.

I noticed a massive difference with the school being a special needs school as they were really geared up to meet every child's needs. They were such amazingly kind staff and very understanding. This would take me a long time to get used to, as in all of my other experiences with schools, I had been made to feel the guilty one, as if I were keeping him off on purpose. At least that's how it felt to me, except for the lovely primary he thrived at for one year with Mrs. Card. I suppose it is so much easier to blame the parents so that they don't have to deal with any issues like EHCP and paperwork to fill in. This school was so much different, and I believe, without a doubt, if he had been able to access this wonderful setting years ago, he would be flying high by now and a very different young man

One morning, Charlie was sick in school, but he did well and gave a small signal that he wanted the toilet room, which for Charlie was the biggest hugest step forward and something that had not been achievable previously. Such a shame that he had been sick, of course, as it set him back again, and he didn't feel like going. Immediately, the old familiar stomach-churning dread in me raised its head in my already fragile mind and body. But this time, when I rang in to tell them, it was different. No drama and no pressure was to be put on either of us. They understood, and what a huge, massive relief that was. From his teacher, to teaching assistants, pastoral care, and the head teacher were all massively supportive.

I had a meeting with the school. I went on my own as, by now, my support worker had moved on, but not until she knew things would be okay for Charlie. This time, I wasn't so nervous about attending a meeting as I knew that they were all wanting the best for Charlie. They were all one hundred percent behind us. "We will not give up on Charlie," said Jade, the pastoral care manager, which Laurie, the deputy head, echoed. It was like music to my ears after so many years of uncertainty. "You won't, will you?" I added just to make absolutely sure that my ears had not deceived me. "We promise," they both smiled and, true to their word, they haven't, which I will come to later.

The next hurdle was the transfer from DLA to PIP. I had filled the forms in great depth (god knows how), gathering evidence from his doctor, CAMHS, CAMHS doctor, osteopath and hospital, and put them in the post-recorded delivery. I was really hoping for a paper-based assessment for Charlie, and along with the forms, I attached a letter from Charlie's psychologist to explain that he would find a face-to-face assessment extremely difficult. So, a paper-based or home visit would be in his best interest. But it was a firm no, twice.

I was very apprehensive as regards to both Kenny and myself for actually getting Charlie to the assessment centre, and of course, it was the one the furthest away from our home! But I dared not rearrange as you only get the opportunity to reschedule twice, and then the claim is discounted, just to add to the pressure! So the dreading morning soon arrived for the assessment and with the promise of a milkshake and McDonald's afterwards, the golden dangling carrot seemed to be working as Charlie got up and dressed, shoes and socks on, which was a very good sign. "Can we have the McDonald's in the car, mum? I don't want to eat in?" Charlie expressed, "Yes, of course, we can," I replied eagerly. We could have eaten it on the top of Mount Snowdon with an entire brass band playing if it got him there.

We arrived at the centre, and very soon, the three of us got called through to a very dark, stuffy, windowless room. Thank goodness Kenny was with us for much-needed support. I had been praying that we would get a nice, understanding assessor. Of course, we didn't! We got the jobsworth and were in that awful room for two hours. She was asking him if he could plan a journey. Charlie looked at me for help, to which I said no, he couldn't plan a journey. "Why not? Haven't you got a mobile, Charlie?" again, he looked at me, "No, he hasn't got a mobile as he doesn't go out, and on the very rare occasion he does, he is with me or a trusted adult." She had an answer for everything. "Well, if mummy got you a mobile, do you think that then you could go on the bus, as you can plan a route for yourself then, now that you are a big boy?" Charlie, of course, nodded yes in agreement, which seemed to please her as she gave a smile in my direction. I told her that Charlie would answer yes or no to questions that he thought were what you wanted to hear, as then it was the end of the conversation. "Okay mummy, well, I am sure Charlie would be truthful with me, won't you Charlie?" He nodded yes again. I reminded her at that point that I am his legal appointee and Charlie has selective autism, so will find all of this very overwhelming.

Then it was the maths questions, add this up and that up, followed by spelling simple words forwards then backwards. Now, Charlie is fairly good at maths and spelling, considering how much time he had missed from school, so he found this section okay, although it took him a long time to do. She was thrilled with this and was rapidly writing her findings down on her pad. "See mummy, isn't he clever?" Argh, if she called me mummy once more, I might well explode. Instead, I cried. I felt very annoyed that I did, but it didn't take much to set me off. But somewhere deep down inside me, I found that old familiar fire in my belly starting to rise. To my surprise, I said, "You know, people who are autistic are very bright.

So, I fail to see why you are asking all these questions. Just because he can spell and do maths doesn't mean his crippling anxiety has suddenly gone away. It doesn't mean that he finds walking and communicating with others near impossible or has some miracle occurred, and he is now fine with no problems. I thought it wasn't about the diagnosis you have but how it affects you on a daily basis and impacts your life. Or have I misunderstood?" She smiled her condescending smile in my direction, but I didn't care. I was just about fed up. It's hard enough looking after a child or any person with additional needs, let alone the constant barriers that you are faced with. The fight for education, fight for getting believed, fight for an EHCP, fight for services; the list goes on.

Thankfully, we left soon after. I smiled and thanked her for being so understanding, sarcastically, I may add. Charlie added, only just out of earshot, "She wasn't very nice, was she mum?" I thought of saying shhh, she will hear you but decided against it, instead saying, "No, she was not." Charlie enjoyed his McDonald's and soon forgot about the experience, unlike us, as the wait for the reply as to whether or not he had been successful was a very long eight weeks. Thankfully, though, it was all okay, and Charlie got awarded. If he hadn't, then I would have asked for what's called an MR (mandatory reconsideration), and if that failed, then it would have to go to appeal, which, of course, we would have done. We didn't come this far for some woman to fail him just because he could spell "moon" and "sport" backwards. Honestly, it beggars belief.

It really sickens me to think that there are not just hundreds but thousands and thousands up and down the country who are going through this on a daily basis. Surely, it's a basic human right to be educated, included, and to feel nurtured and not isolated in a safe environment. As I've said before, if the shoe was on the other foot and I refused my child help or to send him to school, I would soon be in prison, and social services would be involved in a heartbeat. You even get a fine for taking your child out of school during term time to go on holiday! We had to reach a crisis point before we could get proper intense help, and by then, it's very often too late, and the damage is already done and so deep-rooted. School trauma turned into school refusal turns to school phobia, which inevitably turns to self-isolation. It's endless, with lots of knock-on effects that impact the whole family, which is why I was still struggling as to why that horrible man could have taken advantage as he did. I've met a few bad apples over the years, but never one as rotten to the core as him.

I had not heard anything from him at all, that is, until August 2019, two months after I had been to the doctor.

I hadn't been up long. I turned on my phone, and it was then that I was alerted that I had received a private message via Facebook. When I opened the message, it was a blank profile picture, just a white silhouette. The sender of the message called himself Matt Wardle and read as follows:

"Hi Sharon, you do not know me. Matt Wardle is not my real name. I am a county council employee and have been for twenty years. It has recently been drawn to my attention that a young man working with young people in your area has been suspended and is very likely to lose his job next week. I do not know this young man, but as I say, this situation has been drawn to my attention, and I cannot help but to give you the information. The ongoing suspension has had an adverse effect on his life. As well as him essentially losing his job, he has been asked to leave home by his wife and is living in his car. Further information on this is unknown to me. I have not or will not make any contact with him, as I say, I am just passing on information to you as I think you will be interested to hear this."

My arms went numb with pins and needles, and I found it hard to breathe. I was having my first-ever full-blown panic attack. Black dots were forming before my eyes. I had to breathe. Just breathe.

I reported the message immediately as he was not to contact me. I still don't know if it was him, but I found out from a reliable person that nobody of that name worked or had ever worked for the county council. The disciplinary was just days away, and I just know by gut feeling it was him or he was behind it.

On the day of the disciplinary, I was told I would get a phone call to let me know the outcome. Just after 1 pm, my mobile rang, and I was told, "It's over. He has gone." I asked for more details, but due to protecting his confidentiality, I was not allowed to know anything that had gone on or what was said. Ironic, considering this was my life that had been so badly affected. "Can you at least tell me whether or not he admitted what he did to me?" I was told, "No, not all of it. You will be waiting a very long time if you want that to happen."

So, in other words, he would never admit it. The next message that was relayed to me was, "Tell Mrs Jeacock to try and move on with her life and try to get over it. She did the right thing." I remember thinking in my still dazed state, "Oh, that's great then. I can just forget being groomed and abused. Just like that!"

My next step to recovering and getting back to some sort of mental stability, counselling had been arranged for me at OSARCC, a crisis centre in the next city. It was all still so raw for me, as it was still only September 2019, so only three months since I had been to the GP and one month since the disciplinary. I can remember sitting on the bus feeling the most alone that I have ever felt in my life. I still hadn't been able to tell many people, and this is not something that I ever envisaged that I would have to go through, let alone caused by someone in a position of trust.

I entered the room at the centre, and there were around eight other women present, along with two counsellors. The other ladies were all of different ages from all walks of life. We all had one thing in common, though, that brought us all together in that room. We had, in one way or another, been subject to abuse, some historical, some only a few years ago, and then mine, which was weeks ago. The two ladies running the group were so lovely and kind. We would start each session with a guided meditation to help relax us all. I really enjoy meditation as a rule, but in this scenario, the quietness made me think more. It was all I could do just to stop myself from crying, and for those first three or four sessions, that is all I did – just sat very quietly with tears running down my face. "Do you want to take a few moments, Sharon? As I can see, you are really upset," the counsellor asked me. "No, I will be alright, thank you," I managed to squeak out. I knew that if I were to take time out, I would have found it almost impossible to go back into the room. I had visions of all the other faces turning round to look at me when I re-entered the room, and I wasn't sure I could cope with that. In total, we had around ten group sessions to attend. They were a great bunch, and I am still in touch with a few to this day.

I didn't participate very much in the group sessions and remained very quiet throughout. I am not good in groups and would be much better in a one-to-one session, which I was put on the waiting list for. Osarcc is a fantastic, worthwhile charity, and I would not have gotten through those early days without their advice and support.

December 2019 came around, and I was still at an extremely low point and had no zest for life. I was just going through the motions of meeting friends and plastering on a smile. I was constantly asking about their lives to avert any questions they might ask me about mine. On occasions, they would ask, "So, how's things going with you all?" I would casually say, "Yes, fine, just the same old same old," followed up by a laugh and convincing smile then quickly moving on to another topic.

I made another doctor's appointment as, by now, I felt that I needed more help with my mental health while I awaited the one-to-one sessions. That was a huge turning point for me as, alongside the antidepressants that she prescribed me, she also changed my HRT medication. I had been in full-blown menopause for the last eight years, so it was probably due for a change.

After being on the antidepressants for three weeks, I had to go back to my GP so she could see how things were and if I felt as though I was coping a little bit better. I reported to her that I didn't feel that there had been much of an improvement as I was still feeling very low. The doctor upped the antidepressants twice more over the next few weeks, and slowly but surely, my mood started to lift. I noticed that I wasn't crying so much, not every day, at least. I wasn't as tired, and that awful fog of lethargicness was ebbing away. I felt as though getting out of bed wasn't quite as hard as it had been. I felt stronger to help support Charlie and to continue to fight his corner. I hadn't realised just how ill I had become over the last few years until I had a total breakdown and got the help I so needed, along with the unwavering patience and love from Kenny. He really looked after me and continues to in my ongoing recovery. I would not be in the place that I am now without him.

So, whilst I was feeling a bit stronger, my ISVA (Independent Sexual Violence Advisor) had arranged for me to go for an STI check in case 'he' had given me something. I was dreading it and did not want to go, but I knew that I had to. The ISVA wrote a letter for me to give to the nurse, who I have to say was the most adorable, kind, down-to-earth nurse I have ever met. She made a very emotional experience far less traumatic for me, and I could do my own swabs which helped no end. Thank goodness all the tests came back all clear.

I heard from 'him' once more in July 2020, fifteen months after he groomed me. He had found me on Facebook again and private messaged me, only this time using his real name. It read as follows: "Hi Sharon, I know I should not contact you, but my mental health is really struggling. I hardly see my kids, and I have not a penny to my name. I really had feelings for you, but you did me wrong, Sharon, and your life hasn't changed, and you are sitting pretty. Have you told your husband? No, thought not. This isn't about revenge. I just wanted you to know that you have totally destroyed my life, and you are putting nails in my living coffin." He was being delusional and was making out it was all on me. I did reply back saying, "I know exactly what happened and what you did to me, and of course, I have told my husband." His reply certainly showed his true colours. "Bullshit, Sharon, all of this and whatever you think went on is all in your head, and it always has been."

I was feeling stronger now, and although it shook me up and deeply upset me, I was not going to let this man mess with my head. I could see him for what he was. My ISVA told me how to archive the message, so I wouldn't be able to see it, but it would be saved for future reference if needed. I then replied one last time, "I do not want you to contact me anymore; I am now blocking you." That way, if he ever tried to contact me again in the future, this would be classed as harassment and stalking, so this message would prove that I had warned him. All of this, as I said, put me back in my recovery. I was told that this sort of harassment is called gaslighting. I had never heard of gaslighting, but it's basically when the abuser turns it all around on the victim to try and make themselves feel good or to shift the blame off of them.

Horrible, horrible man.

CHAPTER THIRTEEN

September 2019: I still hadn't confided in anyone about what had happened to me. Only Kenny knew, and I felt this dreadful dragging weight upon me that I wasn't the same person at all. My friends were starting to notice the dramatic weight loss and my distance towards them. I felt I didn't want to talk to anyone; it was just too much effort, and I was tired. As part of the healing process, I was encouraged to speak to trusted friends if I felt able to, as, in a way, it would free this guilt that I felt and couldn't shake that I had been so stupid to believe he was a nice person.

I really wanted to confide in my three good friends, but how on earth do you begin to broach a subject of this nature? "Liz would know what to say and help me," I remember thinking. Liz is such a loving, warm person and has always looked out for me. We told each other everything and were so in tune with each other we almost knew what the other was thinking. We had first met when Liz started at the care home I worked in. She was the most nurturing carer, so kind, and nothing was too much trouble for her. I used to think that when I got old, I would love a carer just like Liz to look after me. Liz had the best sense of humour and was a very straight-down-the-line person. What others would think, Liz would say and speak up. If something isn't right, then you could count on Liz to do something about it. I admired that in her and would say, "I wish that I could be more like you and say how I feel and speak out if something is wrong." Liz would always say it in such a calm way and rarely got agitated in the heat of the moment.

"It will come with age, Sharon. I used to be like you and not say anything." Liz was right, and it did come with age, but much, much later for me. I am slowly getting there. The night I told her was just like any other Sunday night. We would go to the village bingo together, and afterwards, we would sit outside and have a cigarette, as it was the only time we really got to talk together and catch up about the week. Liz is the friend that I was doing the spiritual healing course with, and the next week at the group, we were going to be learning some more about all of the chakras and their meanings, colours, and that sort of thing. We were both worried about learning new things, and I was not looking forward to this new project at all. I had already decided that I was going to give the course up as the chakras were just too much of a reminder for me, as that was one of the ways that he used to engage with me. It was just a step too far.

As Liz was talking about all we would have to remember, I just blurted out, "I can't do the course anymore, Liz. I'm sorry, but I am going to give it up. It's just too much for my brain to learn." thinking that would be all I would need to say. "No, no, Sharon, you can't. You have come this far, almost a year and a half. Why?"

"I just can't, Liz, it's the chakras." Then I started to cry; I couldn't hold them back anymore, and I certainly couldn't hide it from her anymore. I managed to tell her in between sobs; poor Liz was so upset, crying, shaking, and so angry. "Why didn't you tell me, Sharon? I could have helped you."

"I didn't tell anyone for months."

In true Liz style, she was amazingly supportive and knew just what to do. She spoke with my permission to our church minister, who was also our trainer doing the course, who was just as understanding as Liz. "You have worked so hard, Sharon; it would be such a shame to forsake it all." she kindly said, just as Kenny had too. I agreed to give it a good think-over and let her know. After some time, I thankfully came to the decision that I wouldn't let him tarnish something that I had always wanted to do and enjoyed doing. So, with some tactful reshuffling of things, I was able to avoid the chakras and the music that had played alongside the healing sessions. We still had music, but not the kind that reminded me of him. For the kindness and thoughtfulness of the minister, I shall never forget and will be forever grateful.

Liz rang me two or three times a week in the early days of me telling her, which really helped keep me focused. We will always have a very special bond. I told my other three closest friends, Emma, Kirsty, and Mel, and they were all just as supportive and amazing as Liz. I really don't know what I would have done without them all, and I just wish that I had told them sooner. I had known Emma for about fifteen years through our children being in the same primary school, and she too had gone through some tough times at the school, so we had lots in common, and we spent a lot of time together. I trusted her implicitly, and she helped me with much-needed advice over the years regarding Charlie. We would go out with another two of the mums maybe once every couple of months or so. It did us all the power of good and was a really much-needed tonic over the years.

Emma was so lovely and didn't push me into anything; just listened and said all the right things. We will always be the best of friends. Melanie was the other of my friends whom I confided in. Mel lives some miles away, and we don't see a lot of each other, not as much as we would like to, as neither of us drives. We would catch up now and again, though, visiting each other by taking the train and meeting up for a meal. I have known Mel for about twenty-five years, and it is a really strong friendship, the sort of friendship you have when you can't always meet, but when you do, it's as if it was only yesterday, a lovely, relaxed, no-pressure friendship. Mel has the kindest, warmest heart and is so caring; she also has a wonderful sense of humour. We only have to look at each other to know what the other one is thinking. Kirsty, I have known all of my life, and we are more like sisters. I felt I could always tell her everything and vice versa. We have such a strong bond and can always be ourselves with each other.

I feel very lucky to have such caring, loyal friends. I have not got loads of friends, but the ones I have got are keepers. There are so many good, genuine people out there in the world. It helps to focus on the good and not the untrustworthy, unsavoury, wicked kind of so-called humans. I've had some much-appreciated help with Charlie over the years, Lorna, Flo, Richard, and Claire, who were a tremendous support to our family as well. I will always remember them and never forget them. I have also met some not-so-nice people over the years, and I shall always remember and never forget them either!

CHAPTER FOURTEEN

In December 2019, I received the outcome from the local government and social care ombudsman. We were all delighted that our investigator had found the county council had been at fault, and at long last, the truth had come out despite the council repeatedly trying to blame me and twist things that I had said. The ombudsman normally only goes back for a year or two regarding complaints, but as ours was so unbelievable, she decided she would go back a further five years. In reality, it was much more than five years and more like ten years that Charlie, by this time, had been out of education. The investigator explained that five years is the absolute limit, and they don't usually go back that far.

The council was found at fault for almost all of the complaints that I had raised, and there are pages and pages of documents with evidence that I had given and which the LGO investigator had proven was right. So, I shall just summarise the outcomes:

Analysis:

In January 2015, the council became aware Y was not attending school regularly. The report completed in April 2015 said that despite a coordinated multi-agency approach, interventions had not enabled Y to attend school regularly. It recommended Y be assessed for an EHCP plan. Despite this report, the council did not request an EHCP plan assessment for Y at this time, and there is no evidence it requested others to do so either. This is a fault.

From September 2015 to July 2016, the council provided Y with weekly support visits at home. The council says it reviewed the effectiveness of this intervention termly, but I have seen no evidence of this. School attendance records show Y was absent for 80% of this academic year, which was an increase from 66% the previous year. Despite this, the council reduced Y's home visits in April 2016.

Although it said it planned to provide more intervention in school instead, this decision cannot have been based on Y's needs, as it was clear Y was still unable to attend school regularly because of their health needs. Y's absence rate from school had increased, but during this academic year, there is no evidence the council considered either:

> The need to try alternative interventions to increase their school attendance;

< The need to provide alternative education as Y had been out of school for over 15 days; or

< Referring Y for an EHCP plan assessment.

This failure to review its intervention, consider the need for an EHCP plan, or provide any alternative education provision despite increasingly poor attendance was a fault.

In October 2016, Y was still not attending school and was signed off by the community mental health team as unfit to attend because of ill health. Council records show it was aware it needed to arrange alternative provisions at this stage, but none was put in place. Y did not receive any education between October and December 2016. Y missed out on half a term of education. This is a fault.

In January 2017, the council agreed to assess Y for an EHC plan. Between January and May 2017, although Y had visits from a support worker at home to try and reduce their anxiety, they did not attend school or receive any education. There is no evidence the council offered or provided any alternative provision. Y missed out on a further one and a half-terms of education. This is a fault.

In June 2017, Y was only able to attend school once between September and December 2017. There is no evidence the council offered or provided Y with any alternative education provision during this time. This is a fault.

The council has partly upheld Mrs X's complaint that it may have been appropriate to call an EHC plan review meeting in December 2017. It gives one of its reasons for not doing so as that it had not been able to evaluate if school B was suitable, as Y had not attended. The fact that Y had not attended school B because of ill health and despite intensive support was precisely the reason a review was needed. The failure to call for an EHC plan review at this time is a fault.

Y did not attend school at all between December 2017 and May 2018. During this time, there is no evidence the council met its statutory duty to provide suitable alternative educational provision. This led to Y missing out on a further one and a half terms of education. This is a fault.

In June 2018, the council reviewed Y's EHC plan, but there is no formal record of this meeting. The officer notes from the EHC plan review meeting record Mrs X's view that Y needed a home tutor. Mrs X says the council agreed to provide this, but the council says this was not the case. The lack of a formal record of this meeting means we now cannot know what was agreed. The failure to keep proper and appropriate records is at fault.

After this meeting, the council did not provide Mrs X with a draft amended EHC plan until December 2018 or issue the final amended EHC plan until February 2019. It should have finalised the amended EHC plan within 8 weeks. This is a 27-week delay and is a fault. The council has accepted this delay as a fault but has not offered Mrs X and Y a remedy.

Mrs X was dissatisfied with the decision not to proceed with home tutoring after June 2018. The delay in issuing the amended EHC plan delayed her opportunity to appeal against the content of the amended plan. This caused further injustice to Mrs X and Y.

The council has accepted it should have put in a home tutor sooner. It said it was working with Mrs X and Y's preference in not doing so.

However, the officers' notes from the EHC plan review in June 2018 record Mrs X's view that Y needed a home tutor at that point. This inconsistency is likely to cause further uncertainty to Mrs X and Y.

Y did not attend school between September 2018 and January 2019. There is no evidence the council provided Y with any alternative education provision until home tutoring began in February 2019. This is a fault.

In total, the council failed to provide alternative education for Y for 9 terms and 1 month between January 2015 and January 2019. Although it did make efforts to support Y to reduce their anxiety and return to school during this time, it did not appropriately review the success of these interventions. It also failed in its duty to provide Y with alternative education while they were unable to attend school because of their health needs.

Our guidance on remedies recommends a financial payment to remedy the impact on a child of a loss of education. Although Y is now receiving home tutoring, they have missed out on a substantial amount of education since 2015 because of the identified faults. It is appropriate to make recommendations in line with our guidance to remedy the injustice caused.

Recommended action:

1. Write to Mrs X and Y to apologise for the identified faults;

2. Pay Mrs X £11,200 to be used for Y's educational benefit. This payment is to remedy the impact on Y of the loss of education between September 2015 and January 2019 and the impact of the delays in the EHC plan process;

3. Pay Mrs X £1,000 to recognise the uncertainty and distress caused to her by the faults;

4. Remind its staff of the importance of keeping proper and appropriate records of meetings.

Within three months of the decision, the council should:

1. Provide evidence of how it has reviewed its procedures related to the timely review of support it provides to children with reduced school attendance;

2. Consider if any further procedural changes are needed to reduce the recurrence of the identified faults. It should provide us with evidence it has done this.

So there it was, all in black and white. I felt like framing it. Some say the compensation should have been so much more, and yes, it should. But to us, it was all about the principle and the injustice it caused to a young, beautiful boy's life that was made unbearable due to the powers that be. It was educational neglect and has had a huge impact on his life—no education, missed opportunities, missed GCSEs, friendships, isolation, isolation for all our family. I was made to feel I lied, and then they twisted things every which way they could backtrack. My son was literally 'out of sight, out of mind'. If this helps just one family in telling our story, then I have at least succeeded in my plight. Never ever give up.

I felt very pleased with the findings and the comfort that, due to these complaints, things will or should change for other families going through similar struggles. And just to raise awareness that you don't always take things at face value and believe all that you are told, like I did.

If something doesn't sit or feel right, then delve deeper and seek advice from advocates or Citizens Advice. There are loads of support groups on Facebook—Not Fine in School, School Phobia and School Refusal, and Parenting Mental Health are just a few I could mention. They are so knowledgeable. I only wish I had come across them before. I had done what I set out to do and finally got some sort of justice for our son.

CHAPTER FIFTEEN

Charlie is in a much calmer place now, still far too traumatised to attend school, but with the unwavering help and support from his special needs school, he can now manage two hours per week with Gary, a pastoral carer and TA, who visits him at our home. They do lots of lovely cooking together, play chess, and go for a walk. Charlie has even progressed to weekly Zoom meetings once a week with Gary to help make him feel included within his class. Gary is so patient, and if Charlie doesn't feel able to do something, then that's fine—proceeding at his own pace takes the pressure off both Charlie and myself, as now I feel I am not letting anybody down, which was something that I always felt when trying to get him to go to other settings.

They are both bonding really well together and building a very good rapport. Charlie still gets very tired after the visits, but now it's more of a contented tired rather than an overwhelming, can't cope, collapsible, worried tired.

On the mornings Gary visits, I wake Charlie up at 7 am in preparation so he can get ready, as it still takes him a huge amount of time. He likes everything to be just so and all in order, ready for his shower. He comes downstairs with no problem; not once has he ever done that on a regular basis... I dare not hardly say that in case of jinxing it!

The school understands that this is going to take a long, long time, as all the years of being first of all in the wrong setting, then moving on to a mainstream school has had a major effect on him, and there is a lot of unravelling to do.

But for our family, that is fine with us, more than fine, as we would rather have the go-slow approach than the gun-ho approach. I always knew that Charlie was capable of achieving things if taken at his speed with the right people and school. I often, over the years, came across staff who would look at me like I had just landed from Mars and grown two heads when I would say, "I can't get him in today." But now he is 100% understood, and he wasn't school refusing (I still hate that word), but he was just not mentally strong enough to go in because of lack of support, failings, and a dismissive head teacher in the past, which is still where I totally believe Charlie's trauma rooted from. It doesn't matter what professionals have read in a book or learned at university; the knowledge of knowing our child and gut feelings far outweigh anything. If only Charlie's original head teacher had listened to his consultant and me and taken her knowledge on board, then we would be in a much different place now. Not listening has been detrimental, damaging, and just ludicrous!

Just because his struggles weren't so apparent in school does not mean it wasn't there. Astronomers are still finding new stars in space, but they have always been there, like planets just undiscovered.

People say, "We didn't have all this autism back in our day." Yes, you did, but it wasn't recognised then and put down to bad behaviour or a bit odd, a bit of a loner, eccentric. Very often, these poor people were locked away in asylums, care homes, and even prisons. I am sure now, looking back, that when I was a carer in the home, we had several residents in our care that I would now definitely say had autistic traits. Some were very quiet and seldom talked, some wouldn't stop talking in an over-enthusiastic way, and some were very, very regimented and a stickler for time. I remember one gentleman I used to care for had the most dreadful leg ulcers which would need cleaning and dressing daily. It used to worry him like anything if they weren't done by 10 am, and he would be standing outside his door waiting for me. I would rush by, having been called away to another resident, signalling to him with my fingers, "Five minutes, and I will be with you." Well, very often, that five minutes would turn into thirty minutes, and by the time I had got to him, he was not best pleased with me, tapping with his finger on his wristwatch impatiently. He never spoke in all the years I looked after him and would signal with his hands and arms what he wanted. He was a lovely man who just preferred his own company.

Another lady would get incredibly anxious if we hadn't gone to the day room at 8 pm to collect her in her wheelchair to take her to her room to get her ready for bed, the same in the morning, and had to be one of the first up. If we were the slightest bit late, she would be ringing her bell, worked up in a terrible state. We really tried to accommodate the times that she liked, but when you have around forty other residents all wanting to get up or go to the toilet, sometimes things do run over.

Back then, of course, autism didn't even enter my head. I had heard of it but never encountered anyone with it... or had I? The old cliché hindsight is a wonderful thing that certainly springs to mind.

So things here at home were altogether much better. Then COVID-19 struck. Our first thought was it won't come here, don't worry. But as we all know now, it most certainly did. First, miles away, then slowly edging closer until you actually knew of people locally who had caught it and been very seriously ill. It came to our village, and a few people had it and, thank goodness, recovered. Sadly, one man we knew didn't make it, and a young woman who was so vibrant, cheerful, and full of life sadly succumbed to it after a tremendous fight. Just devastating. I prayed for my friends and residents at the care home and all the doctors and nurses on the front line as we all did. They are so brave, putting their lives on the line day in and day out. Shop workers, bank staff, supermarket staff, cleaners, paramedics, and so many more that are very often overlooked. Suddenly, it all got very real.

Kenny was furloughed from his job for a couple of months. We all worried about him going back as he is classed as a key worker and had to work a lot in hospitals, and some jobs were on the COVID wards. His boss was really cautious and made sure that they all had good-grade PPE. Nevertheless, it was still a huge worry for us all. Joseph was still working and cooking food for the NHS, which would get distributed to the local hospitals. I would make both Kenny and Joseph take their shoes and clothes off just inside the door and put them in the wash straight away. We would put a post outside to decontaminate and wash our hands constantly. I still did the weekly shop with Kenny driving me and waiting in the car. I would get increasingly cross with the number of people not wearing their masks correctly, with their noses hanging out! What is the point of that, I would think, people not respecting social distancing and leaning over me trying to get their favourite cheese or something? I would sigh very loudly, "Can you give me my space, please?" pushing my trolley between us as some sort of guard. I would never have been so bold before.

As for life in regards to Charlie and myself, though, things remained just the same. We had been isolated for years, so we were well-trained in this. I weirdly felt some comfort in the fact that, just for once, we were the same as everybody else and had to stay in, not go to work, and not see friends on a spur-of-the-moment whim.

People were starting to really suffer from mental health issues, which I can relate to. We felt safe and sheltered at home, though. Not everybody could feel safe, and nobody knows what people go through behind closed doors. Maybe work was their only escape from life at home.

I busied myself baking and walking my beloved companion Fern on our allowed daily exercise. I felt worried about coming out of lockdown for fear of catching COVID and unwittingly passing it on to my family. I felt content at home and could always find plenty of things to do. Of course, my counselling had been put on hold, understandably. I was offered Zoom sessions with others, but that really isn't something I felt like doing. I would much rather wait and talk one-on-one when the time comes. My doctor was always at the other end of the phone should I ever feel I needed her, which was a great comfort.

Of course, I missed my friends, but we always kept in touch either by phone, text, or messenger. Not the same, I know, but it will feel all the more special when we can meet. Gary could still visit Charlie, thank goodness, as he is classed as vulnerable and has the EHCP so that stayed the same. Charlie is still very regimented and always will be. That's fine, though, as long as he is happy. He prefers his own company in his bedroom; it's his sanctuary. I still long for the day for us all to go out as a family, nothing grand, just a little walk or trip to the cinema, a meal out. It almost feels like a loss, and we have all missed out on so many things over the years that others take for granted, just the simple little things. Some days are still challenging and incredibly hard, but I am more in control of 'me now, and if I am having a bad, low day, that's fine. Some days, I am shattered, and it takes all my time to force myself out of bed. I am fine once up and can do my jobs in the house, but come the afternoon, that's when it hits me, and all my energy has depleted. I have accepted that now and don't feel guilty for resting. A lady once said to me, "If all you do is make your bed in a day, that's okay. Always have a nicely made bed to get into at bedtime."

I have a good day if Charlie has a good day, which I am very pleased to say is more often than not. Charlie's cheeky smile and sense of humour are slowly returning, and all I want to do is squeeze him. No chance, though. He has his spark returning.

At the moment, we are awaiting an appointment with the orthopaedic specialist as his hypermobility is worse, he is very flat-footed, and his toes have fused straight, which makes walking very painful. He has had built-up insoles in the past, but this time may mean an operation, which would immobilise him for three months. He took it all in his stride, though, and is really keen to have the surgery to stop the pain.

Now that Charlie is eighteen, he will be discharged from CAMHS, and his GP will take over prescribing his medication. We have been told that Charlie does not meet the criteria for adult mental health, which I feel is wrong. As I've mentioned before, how ill do you have to be? CAMHS, on the whole, have been good over the years. The doctor at CAMHS was really good and very understanding. However, they are extremely stretched, and I feel that they need to offer more consistency and not just discharge the young person after a few weeks if the problems are still impacting them. The only reason that we were kept on longer is because Charlie is on medication, and the doctor there had to monitor him every few months. Charlie will hopefully have a social worker who can look at ways to support him as he moves on to the next stage of his life and prepares for adulthood. CAMHS cannot discharge him until something is put in place, so that is of some comfort. Charlie's medication changed a couple of years ago, and he is now on sertraline and sleep medication called melatonin, which helps him so much.

Charlie's future will always be not far from my mind, as you always have to be thinking and researching the next steps and stages of the future. We want to make sure that Charlie can be as independent as possible with someone on hand should he need them when Kenny and I are no longer around. Morbid, I know, but if we have learned one thing over the years, it is that you can't always rely on people's words, so we need things legally in place. I am not just advocating for his education, care, and health; I'm advocating for his future, and I will not compromise this time. I may have had an apology from the local authority, and things will have hopefully changed for other children and parents, and there won't be such a fight for everyone, as an apology without change is pointless. I want words matching actions this time. I have clued myself up on some of the laws regarding what must happen, and if it doesn't, then I would not hesitate to speak out loud and clear. Parents shouldn't be silenced and made to feel a nuisance; our knowledge of our children far outweighs anything.

I wish that Charlie's original head teacher had listened to his consultant and myself, as not taking our knowledge on board has been detrimental, damaging, and plain ludicrous! I won't pretend that this has affected us all as a family because it has immensely. Just because we carry it well doesn't mean it doesn't hurt. No family should have to go through this, and yet there are thousands out there in the same position. Yet when COVID hit, people were up in arms as children had missed out on a few months of education; try years.

In myself, I am feeling stronger most days, but I will never be the same person that I was before that man groomed me. I have some wonderful friends who I have told about what happened, three trusted friends, Liz, Emma, and Melanie, whom I have known for a very long time, and we have always been there for each other over the years.

Their reactions were all of shock, anger at him, and wonders of why I didn't confide in them sooner as they would have been there for me and helped me. Their understanding was limitless, and for that, I will always be grateful. I so wish I had told them at the time, but how on earth do you bring that topic up? Where do you start?

It is all part of my healing process and just makes me realise how dreadfully depressed I had become over the years. I have come to realise that my tears were not a sign of weakness; it was, in fact, me trying to be strong for far too long. I guess I had just got so used to feeling like that it became me – all smiles and cheerful conversation on the outside, but the most awful dark feeling on the inside. And it very nearly tipped me over the edge in what he put me through. I still, and probably always will, hold great contempt for him and what he did to me – bad enough for any man to do that, but a man in that position, I just can't fathom. It really does make me second-guess people now. I am not a forgiving person and never have been. They say you should forgive as it can help with moving on, but I know that will never happen for me. I can move on in myself, but I will never let that go. I am like a dog with a bone, which I think is also a good trait and spurs me on even more to fight for what is right for Charlie.

As part of the group counselling I had back in 2019, we were each given a journal in which to write down our personal feelings if we felt that we wanted to. So, that's when I started just to jot down feelings and thoughts that were going through my mind. I found that writing really helped me to get my feelings out, and that journal was very quickly filled up, so I brought another bigger journal. Likewise, that was also filled with thoughts and feelings, and very soon, I had filled three journals.

Throughout the lockdown, I noticed that some people were making use of the extra time and making some wonderful artwork, decorative cakes, photography, and many other newfound hobbies. That is what inspired me to hopefully turn my journal into a book. If this could help even one family to feel that they are not alone in this journey, then I could at least feel I have contributed and raised much-needed awareness on the minefield of special educational needs and the knock-on mental health needs that can be incurred.

This isn't meant to be a sad memoir, but more, one of hope and determination that you are not alone in this battle. I have found comfort and very knowledgeable advice from the parenting mental health group and school refusal support service for phobia, refusal, and separation anxiety. Both are on Facebook. It is, of course, sad that there are so many families going through this, and I am still surprised that there are thousands in just these two groups mentioned. Lots more groups that are out there, too, just a drop in the ocean.

My foremost advice would be never ever give up, and more importantly, never be worried to ask for help if you are struggling and always, always trust your gut instinct. If you have the slightest inkling that your child is displaying unusual behaviour, no matter how young, get that ball rolling as soon as you can.

I hope this resonates with you and can help. You are not alone; you are doing an amazing job, and your child and family are 'the most important thing, so don't worry about speaking out.

I am much more direct in meetings now and just keep in my mind my beautiful caring young man and think of how far he has come. They can go home after a meeting and not give my family a second thought until the next stage. We go home and live with the most precious child, and of course, we want the best we can for them.

CHAPTER SIXTEEN

Charlie has found a new hobby which is target shooting; a family friend mentioned it in passing that they go, and maybe Charlie could come along to see if he liked it. I had my doubts as it would be such a huge thing for him to undertake, as it would mean leaving the sanctuary of his bedroom and venturing outdoors. It just so happens that this family friend who suggested it is one that Charlie is extremely fond of. So, Kenny and I mentioned it to Charlie to see what he thought, and amazingly, he nodded, indicating his keenness to give it a go. What a great suggestion it proved to be. Charlie took to it immediately and was allowed to use the club's rifle for a few weeks to help him get a feel for it. He never faltered in wanting to go! He would get up, shower, dress, and put his shoes and socks on every Sunday morning.

So once we knew that he was serious about his hobby, we took him to choose his own air rifle. Charlie has such a good, keen eye for target shooting and rarely misses the target. He has gone on to win several trophies in many competitions that his dad has entered him, which boosted his confidence to no end. It was lovely to witness him quietly enjoying himself. He wasn't so keen on the presentation part where all of the others would clap and cheer for him when his name got called out. "Well done, Charlie," they would all echo. Charlie would grin shyly and go red but would go up to the front to collect his trophy or medal and shake the chairman's hand—a massive thing for Charlie to do and to overcome. It made us burst with pride.

They were all a great bunch of men and women who all understood Charlie's preference not to talk. They would just say,

"Hi Charlie, alright?" which made a huge difference. He has now even started to say "hi" back to them, another step forward.

Charlie is still engaging very well with Gary, his teacher. He's still not feeling up to going to school but continues to manage walks and make some very tasty meals with Gary. Other days he ventures downstairs to have a play or cuddle with Fern, which the dog laps up. Dogs really do have a very special way of them knowing how to bring you happiness and a smile.

There is still a long way to go in getting Charlie back to being more of his old self, and we all know that it will take time. But with the right help and support, then I know that it is achievable. And if that takes a year or several years, I have no doubt that with Charlie's determination, he will get there.

Charlie is content and much calmer these days. He still has his bad days, grumpy and snappy and impossible to talk to, but then what teenager isn't? On the good days, we all take the time to enjoy it and to remind ourselves just how far things have moved on. It may seem like very small progress, but nonetheless, it is progress.

Our hope for Charlie's future is, as it has always been, for him to be as independent as he can be. Hopefully, go to college if the right ongoing support is in place or maybe get a part-time job with help. Most importantly, to be happy in life. At present, Charlie is receiving great support from a special needs college and has two brilliant support workers who are working closely with him.

Charlie will always need help and support, which is fine, and I will continue to advocate for him. One thing I know for sure, though, is that we will never ever go back to those dreadful, awful years. This time, I will speak louder and fight for him for the rest of my life, and I will do it gladly. Things are still in need of drastic improvement where SEN is concerned, and children/young adults and their families are still being let down and failed massively. Every single thing you have to fight for and justify why you are fighting. You feel like a lawyer by the time you are done and not the normal mum you should be!

Joseph is doing really well and has an apprenticeship to become a site manager. He has always kept his fantastic sense of humour, and I can always rely on him to make me smile no matter what. He always puts things into perspective for me and gives brilliant advice, much more advanced than his years. He knows just what to say and is very calming, a wonderful, kind, and caring young man. We could burst with pride when we think of how far he has come despite his dyslexia with pure determination.

Kenny is my absolute rock and is also extremely caring. When Charlie is having a bad day, and I am upset, he can make me see things from a totally different angle. I am so grateful for all of his love, support, and understanding when I am not always in a very good place, which is thankfully much less than it used to be. Kenny works unbelievably hard and is the most selfless person that I have ever met, and always by my side when I need him the most. My mum is also a great support to all of us, always so thoughtful and kind. If it weren't for my mum, then I wouldn't be able to go out shopping once a week in town as she always stays with Charlie. We go on some lovely long walks together with Fern, as Kenny is on hand at weekends.

Walks have been and continue to be my lifesaver, as even on the days when a walk is the very last thing that I feel like doing, I have to because of Fern. Once I am out in nature and just listening to the birds singing or just taking a moment to myself, it works wonders for my mental health, and I feel so much better for it.

As for the future, who knows? I would like to go back and work in a care home. They were some of the best years of my working life. When I look back on those happy, carefree days in the nursing home and all of the great times we had, it makes me feel hopeful that maybe one day I can return.

We all had some very good times, not only in working together but also get-togethers outside of work. We went out for birthday meals, Christmas dinners, and the once-a-month disco in the village was always something we looked forward to. We would dance the night away, and it was always a late night, but regardless, we would always be back at work at six-thirty the following morning, albeit a bit worse for wear and bleary-eyed. Nothing a sweet cup of tea and a round of hot buttered toast couldn't sort out. Goodness knows how on earth we did it; I couldn't do it now, that's for sure. Fantastic times and sad times as well when, inevitably, a resident would pass away. We loved all of the residents like our own family, and of course, there would always be one that we would get attached to, and that would make it harder to say goodbye. If their family were unable to sit with them in these final hours, then we carers would take turns holding their hand to ensure they were not on their own when the time came. Very sad but also very humbling that we were able to be part of their passing and to be able to perform the last offerings for them, one last final act of care.

One thing I learned is that we all come into this world the same way, and we will all leave this world in the same way. We all need to be washed and fed when we are firstborn, and we will need the same when we are near the other end of life. We are weak as babies; we will be weak and need help walking when we are elderly.

Life is precious and very short. I did qualify as a healing practitioner. I was on the verge of giving it all up, but with the kindness of the minister and her husband and the unbelievable support from Liz, I got through it and managed to pass my exams.

I am still on my antidepressants, and I am in no rush to get off of them yet. Mental health is very important to me now, more than I ever realised it would be. While on the surface, I may have appeared to have been coping and carrying it well, that does not mean it isn't heavy to bear and carry around with you day in and day out. So please, again, if you or anyone you know are struggling or feeling low, just remember there is help out there from your doctor, Samaritans, or other helplines. You are being so strong when seeking help for the first time; that really is the hardest step. You are strong, amazing, and loved by family and friends, and there is always someone that can help, no matter how impossible you think that is. Stay strong, fight for what you believe in, always ask twice if someone is okay, more so if you have noticed that they have been quiet of late and not quite themselves.

As my dear dad would always say, "Don't let them grind you down!" More than likely, a swear word would have been added in there, but I shall leave that bit for your imagination!

Epilogue

I would like to mention the people who have been with me and my family through these difficult years. I am sure that without them, things would not have panned out in the more positive way that they have.

Not all the people mentioned will know everything that has happened, but each and every one of you has made this journey more bearable. The amazing autism advisory team, Richard, Flo, and Lorna, without your calming ways with Charlie, I am sure that things would have been even more intolerable for him. Richard and Flo, so calm and reassuring, and Lorna, with your fantastic sense of fun and humour, each one of you brightened our days.

Gary, Jade, Laurie and all of the staff at the wonderful special needs school who are all so devoted to the students, and all do an amazing job. You are fantastic, caring people.

Liz, Emma, Kirsty, and Melanie, four of my best friends, always at the end of the phone and never ever letting me down. I didn't always feel like engaging or have the mental energy to, but one talk with each of you really lifted me more than you will ever know. I love you all, and you will always be close to my heart.

My beautiful, kind, caring mum, whom I can always rely on to help me where she can. Kenny, for always being my strength and go-to man. Your love, patience, and kindness have brought us even closer together, and I know I wouldn't be in the place I am now without your unconditional love.

Joseph, just for being you! Never change and keep that beautiful, kind nature and sense of humour.

And, of course, Charlie, who may not know it but has shown me so much over the years and has opened my eyes in wonder at how far he has come and his determination to keep persevering in life. You will get there, Charlie, and we will all be right beside you to help and encourage you to lead a happy, independent life. Always.

By Sharon Jeacock.

THE END

Printed in Great Britain
by Amazon